ARCHITECTURE
AS ART

Ceiling, entrance hall, Louis Kahn's Yale Center for British Art. (Photograph: George Cserna)

Stanley Abercrombie
ARCHITECTURE AS ART

ICON EDITIONS

HARPER & ROW, PUBLISHERS, New York
Cambridge, Philadelphia, San Francisco, London
Mexico City, São Paulo, Singapore, Sydney

A hardcover edition of this work was originally published in 1984 by Van Nostrand Reinhold Company Inc. It is here reprinted by arrangement with the author.

First Icon paperback edition published 1986.

Library of Congress Cataloging-in-Publication Data

Abercrombie, Stanley.
   Architecture as art.

   (Icon editions)
   Reprint. Originally published: New York : Van Nostrand Reinhold, c1984.
   Includes index.
   1. Architecture—Aesthetics. I. Title.
NA2500.A394   1986   720'.1   85-45780
ISBN 0-06-430159-1 (pbk.)

86 87 88 89 90 HAL 10 9 8 7 6 5 4 3 2 1

Contents

Acknowledgments   6

Introduction: Architecture as Art   7
The Size of Architecture   15
The Shape of Architecture   37
The Shapes within Architecture   55
Placement   87
Function   99
Perception   117
The Meaning of Architecture   125
Architectural Order   147
Conclusion: Three Relationships   165

Index   173

Acknowledgments

This book had its beginnings in a seminar, "Evaluating Architecture," that I taught at the Harvard Graduate School of Design in 1974–75 while there as a Loeb Fellow in Advanced Environmental Studies. Some of the same material was revised for a more general audience as a series of lectures, "The Esthetics of Architecture," at the Smithsonian Institution in 1981. It reached its present form at the American Academy in Rome in 1982–83 where I enjoyed a Mid-Career Fellowship in Architecture funded by the National Endowment for the Arts.

I am grateful to all these institutions, to the kind friends who helped me find my way into them, and to the other friends who helped me once I was there.

I am particularly grateful to Edgar Kaufmann, jr., who read an early version of some sections of the manuscript and suggested fundamental clarifications, and to Ann Ferebee, who offered very thoughtful suggestions at a later stage.

Peter Blake, who gave me my first full-time job as a writer about architecture, has continued to supply generous help and encouragement. To Don Canty, Editor of *Architecture*, I am grateful for much kind support and friendship. And for early and continuing inspiration, for many fine dinners and much good conversation, I will always be grateful to Jim and Mariana Edwards.

S.A.

Introduction: Architecture as Art

Architecture is frozen music.

> Friedrich von Schelling, *Philosophy of Art*

But music is not melted architecture.

> Susanne K. Langer, *Problems of Art*

A book about architecture is one of the few books that can be read inside its subject. Even if a reader is not within a work of architecture, such a thing is likely to be down the street, in the nearest city, or fresh in the reader's mind, for architecture is the most familiar of all arts. Its very familiarity obscures our vision of it as an art, for we know so many things about architecture that are extraneous to art: We may know its location and the building it replaced, its insurance rates and mortgage payments, its occupants and its furniture, how well its air conditioning works and how often its floors are swept. We cannot escape the burden of this esthetically irrelevant information any more easily than we can escape architecture itself.

We may, if we like, avoid all but a glimpse of painting, switch channels at the first step of ballet, and choose to read no poetry, but architecture, as has often been said, is the unavoidable art. It is not only scattered all over the landscape but also likely to stay there a long time. We not only see it often but we also use it; it has been built for a purpose.

Sometimes it has been built for two purposes: to shelter a function and to generate a profit. It could, therefore, also be said to be our most mercenary art form. As Edgar Kaufmann, jr., wrote in *Architectural*

Forum in 1969, "All the oil wells of Arabia will not sweeten this little art; its origins lie in the needs, the whole range of needs, of its animal users." And of its animal owners and developers. Architecture, unlike some other arts, cannot dissent from the opinions of those who would commission it, for it cannot come into existence without such commissions.

But if it often serves venal ends, it can also serve ideals. Architecture can manifest goals of social reform—of more efficient hospitals, more humane factories, more democratic housing clusters, more harmonious relationships between man and nature—and, at its most potent, it can help effect those goals.

Architecture is social in another sense as well: We never see it alone, but always in community with other members of an urban group or in community with nature. A novel, an opera, or a painting can create, for a time, a world of its own. Architecture can cast an equally powerful, equally absorbing spell, but it does so in collaboration with the building next door or the ones down the block, with the way we approach it, with the relationship between its form and the shape of the mountain in the distance, and with the way the sunlight and the shadows of trees fall across its face.

Architecture is complicated not only because of where it is built and why it is built, but also because of the simple fact that it is built. It is not the work of a single artist alone but the product of a large team. "A great building is the greatest conceivable work of art," Henry James thought, "because it represents difficulties annulled, resources combined, labour, courage, and patience." A great building does indeed represent such accomplishments, but these do not make it the greatest conceivable work of art, only the most unlikely. When building becomes art, it does so only by standing on the shoulders of engineering, physics, mechanics, logistics, economics, and craft.

Its familiarity, its practicality, its frequent commercialism, and its intimate ties to society and to its physical surroundings—all these are basic attributes of architecture, but they are not esthetic attributes. We do not consider a building to be a work of art because its elevators are fast or because it turns a neat profit for its developer; yet, as in no other art, the esthetic criteria for architecture are entangled with such mundane matters. Disentangling them is the aim of this book.

Still another obscuring factor is the sad fact that there is so little construction worthy of being called architecture. Some paintings are better than other paintings, obviously, and many fail as art, but unless we include something as foreign in intent as sign painting, we can say that there are no paintings that do not *try* to be art. The situation in building construction is very different: Most buildings have no intention and no hope of being art.

Intent is a prerequisite. "If we wanted to say something about art that we could be quite certain was true," philosopher Richard Wollheim has written in *On Art and the Mind*, "we might settle for the assertion that art is intentional. And by this we would mean that art is something we do, that works of art are things that human beings make." This is particularly true of architecture: there is no such thing as spontaneous or accidental architecture. It comes into being only as the end product of a tedious and expensive process that requires forethought and effort. Even vernacular "architecture without architects" is planned. The thatched *rondavels* of South Africa, the stone *trulli* of southern Italy, the mud huts of the Dogon ("among the greatest sculptors of the world," according to architect Aldo van Eyck) — all these building forms have evolved through processes of trial and error, of gradual improvement and adaptation to climate and function; and, in all cases, the process of their construction is begun with a clear vision of the desired result.

Intent, however, is not enough; our cities are littered with failed intentions. What is it, then, that distinguishes architecture from mere building? This is a question often asked, and there is an obvious answer: Architecture is building raised to the level of art. But it is an answer that leads immediately to another question: What is art? For this one, there are libraries of answers to choose from, but consider just one, an idea about art in the final sentence of Victorian critic Walter Pater's *The Renaissance*: "For art comes to you proposing frankly to give nothing but the highest quality to your moments as they pass, and simply for those moments' sake."

Perhaps because Pater also wrote, in another context, of "love of art for its own sake," his idea has been said to support the discredited ideal of "art for art's sake," but, on the contrary, it supports art for our own sake, for the sake of the quality of our lives. It is a position that needs no apology.

If we accept as fact that building can be raised from its crib of venality and become a contributor to an enhanced life, that at its best it can thrill us and stretch our imaginations and offer us moments of quality as any other art can do, then the next step in understanding the nature of architecture is to consider how it affects us in ways *not* like any other art.

There are principles of design that are common to many arts, from flower arranging to opera, principles of harmony, rhythm, balance, transition, climax, and relief. These are well understood, and their application to architecture important and obvious. Yet each artistic medium has, as well, its own private ways, quite apart from its own private tools. What are the ways special to architecture? Within which characteristics of a building are we to search for the quality that separates good from bad, that elevates construction to art?

These are not questions that deal with periods, regions, or styles. Some aspects of architecture, of course, are rooted in a particular situation and could not withstand intercultural travel. The elaborate iconography of a Gothic cathedral might be largely incomprehensible to a Muslim, and the plan of some traditional Chinese houses, proceeding courtyard by courtyard from the public realm to increasingly private ones, would make no sense in the absence of traditional Chinese etiquette. But these aspects of architecture—didacticism in the first case, the manifestation of social patterns in the second—give us no clue to the *quality* of the built form that supports them. They are esthetically neutral and therefore peripheral to our consideration of architecture as art.

Much writing and thinking about architecture is concerned with permutations of style, with the detection of new trends and with the tracing of their origins. This is the substance of architectural history—distinctions, for example, between the buildings of Republican Rome and Imperial Rome, or among the characteristics of High Renaissance, mannerism, and the baroque. Even in the consideration of current architecture, much attention is spent on labels, classifications, and derivations. The prolific writer Charles Jencks carries such efforts to an extreme in his encyclopedic *Architecture Today*, written in collaboration with William Chaitkin. Jencks distinguishes between "Late-Modernism" and "Post-Modernism" and, within each of these two groups, further distinguishes six sub-groups such as "Extreme Articulation" and "Slick-Tech," and, still further, charts the progress of each of the dozen sub-groups from 1960 to 1980. Such efforts are not without usefulness and certainly not without interest but, again, they deal with aspects of architecture that are peripheral to its value as art. Even if Jencks convinces us that Marcel Breuer's Whitney Museum and Jörn Utzon's Sydney Opera House share the sub-group "Sculptural Form," we have learned nothing about the quality of either the museum or the opera house.

How, then, shall we begin to look for the basis of this art? First of all, we must not look for too much. We must not hope to find—we would not even want to find—a set of criteria so objective and complete that it constituted an exact prescription for either the production or the recognition of art. In art there will always remain some part that is personal and unpredictable.

We do know that architecture's power to move us is unlike that of any other art. It cannot fairly be described as three-dimensional painting, nor as habitable sculpture, nor, certainly, as frozen music. Therefore we must look for a basis peculiar to this art alone.

We know, too, that architecture's power now is the same as it has been throughout all our history. The burial mounds and ceremonial causeways of ancient Egypt, its surfaces and engaged columns, its passages and shadowy niches, all intrigue and touch us in much the same way they must have intrigued and touched their builders. Even if we put completely from our minds whatever we may know of Egyptian religion, Egyptian economy, and Egyptian society—even then these constructions will not cease to speak to us, and their language is the eternal language of architecture. We may or may not be aware that beyond a pair of great pylons lay a sacred precinct to which only a pharaoh and his priests were granted admission; no matter, for the pylons themselves still communicate vividly their role of marking the entrance to uncommon ground.

There must be, then, some constant basis for the art of architecture, continuing intact through all possible changes in technology, in style, and in ourselves. James Marston Fitch is perfectly right in noting that "science and technology have forever altered the scope of the architect's task"; nevertheless, they have done nothing to alter the parts of the architect's work that determine that work's value as art.

We dare not completely neglect aspects of function and context in our investigation, however, for, although they are not esthetic aspects themselves, they contribute to the particular nature of architecture and may well impinge in some way on the basis of judgment we seek. We can also use these aspects as boundaries of our search, making sure that what we find is not destructive of them. It is fine for art to be amoral, but not immoral. It cannot be highly valued and supported if it is inimical to the more prosaic duties of its own medium. It should never exist at the expense of practical, inartistic concerns, but in addition to them.

Within these limits, we hope to be able to find in architecture some manner or characteristic or relationship, no matter how vague or subjective, that is attached only to esthetic quality. Sir Herbert Read seems to have had it in sight when he wrote of "that being-in-itself which exceeds being-for-a-purpose." The basis we seek, being itself unchanging, is not likely to be found in the building's relationship to

Trulli, the conical limestone houses of Italy's Apulia region, idiomatic, but not undesigned. (Photograph: Norman F. Carver, Jr., AIA.)

transient phenomena; it will more likely be found within the building itself and within those ways in which it relates to the permanent aspects of nature, including human nature.

We might reasonably object that the qualities we perceive in any object are never inherent in the object at all but in the response apparatus that we, as observers and users, bring to it. Composers, painters, or architects never complete an art work; they can only offer us material that we will be able to perceive for ourselves as art. But there is a difference between what we perceive in the work the artist gives us and what we perceive in that work's complex and changeable intercourse with its particular context of time and place. It is perception of this second, transitory type that enables us to make use of objects; but it is perception of the first and lasting type that enables us to make art of them.

The Size of Architecture

No perfect thing is too small for eternal recollection.
> Arthur Symonds, introduction to Coleridge's *Biographia Literaria*

On the other hand,

Mere size has, indeed, under all disadvantages,
some definite value . . .
> John Ruskin, *Mornings in Florence*

Gaining a mountaintop, or turning the corner at Sunset and Vine, we confront an object. Our first analysis, so fleet that it is subconscious, is of the object's nature: Is it threatening or benign, alive or inanimate, rushing toward us or stationary? In the same subconscious instant we judge the object's size, using our own size as the measure: Is it smaller than we are, or bigger? If bigger, how much bigger?

So fundamental and habitual are these questions about size, asked in the interest of self-preservation, that we naturally resist the suggestion that size alone can be a source of esthetic pleasure. Part of becoming a civilized adult, after all, is learning the lesson that quality is independent of quantity, and even that quantity may conflict with quality. If we are sensitive to the limits of earthly resources, E. F. Schumacher has told us, we must see that "small is beautiful," and to choose the largest package under the Christmas tree is a display not only of greed but, probably, also of poor judgment. It may be

Atop Kitt Peak in Arizona, the Kitt Peak Observatory by Skidmore, Owings & Merrill: The size of a building, relative to man, plays a crucial role in its effect on us. (Photograph: Ezra Stoller © ESTO)

that in most arts such divorce of size from value is justified: A short story can be, at least arguably, as fine as a novel, a miniature as beautiful as a mural. But size plays an important part in determining the very nature of architecture.

Architecture is our biggest art. It is necessarily larger than ourselves, for it offers spaces for our use. But size is more than just a customary attribute of architecture; it is a basic source for some of the pleasure we derive from this art. We know empirically that this is true when we consider our reactions to, say, Amiens Cathedral, the Roman Colosseum, or the Eiffel Tower. These same buildings, if reduced to a tenth or a hundredth of their size, would lose not just quantity but also quality: Their power over our emotions would be substantially weakened.

Similarly, Le Corbusier was enthusiastic in his admiration for American grain elevators. He illustrated his book *Towards a New Architecture* with photographs of nine groups of them, and he wrote that "simply guided by the results of calculation (derived from the principles which govern our universe) and the conception of a living organism, the engineers of today make use of the primary elements and . . . provoke in us architectural emotions and thus make the work of man ring in unison with universal order." Yet these structures are simple cylinders in shape; if smaller, they could serve as wastebaskets, bollards, or umbrella stands. It is their simple shape *in combination with their size* that excited Le Corbusier.

In buildings that preceded the technological developments of the nineteenth century, size could be equated with mass. Mass alone, in the form of a mountain or in the form of an invented structure, has an ability to impress itself upon our imaginations. As John Ruskin wrote, rather grudgingly, in *The Seven Lamps of Architecture,*

> There is a crust about the impressible part of men's minds which must be pierced through before they can be touched to the quick; and though we may prick at it and scratch it in a thousand separate places, we might as well have left it alone if we do not come through somewhere with a deep thrust. . . . And mere weight will do this; it is a clumsy way of doing it, but an effectual one, too; and the apathy which cannot be pierced through by a small steeple, nor shone through by a small window, can be broken through in a moment by the mere weight of a great wall.

Novelist Elizabeth Bowen, writing specifically about the Aurelian Wall in *A Time in Rome,* said that "substantiality is in itself a beauty.

The Great Pyramid of Cheops, Giza: The power of a simple form built at great size. (Photograph: Stanley Abercrombie)

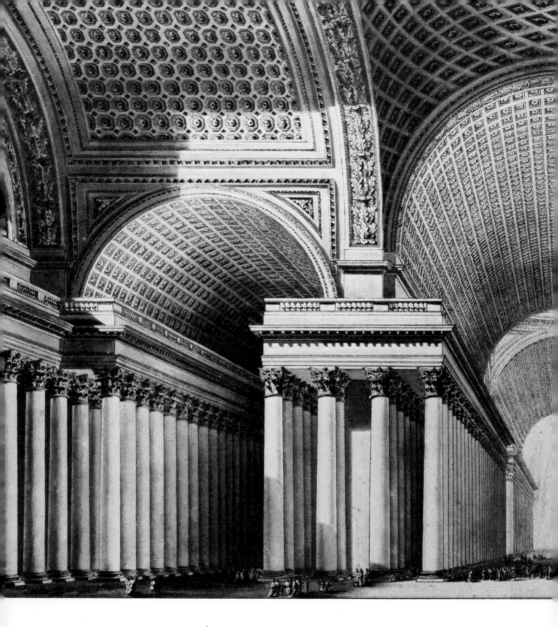

An imaginary interior by Étienne-Louis Boullée: Its impact is due to its cavalier disregard for "human scale." (Photograph: Royal Institute of British Architects)

To brush up against the Wall, or to press one's hand against any part of its surface, is a pleasure." The architectural visionary Buckminster Fuller charged that "most architects haven't the slightest idea how much their buildings weigh," but this is true only in the most literal way; in a way more significant for the results of their work, architects are profoundly conscious of weight, and of substantiality, as sources of pleasure.

(And not just pleasure. Art has more to offer us than pleasure alone; its most striking effects are those we might call, with Edmund Burke, "sublime" rather than beautiful, and the factor of magnitude is often

A passage near Santa Maria della Pace, Rome: The substantiality of a wall can in itself give satisfaction. (Photograph: Stanley Abercrombie)

Two views of James Stirling's Cambridge University History Faculty Building:
No heavy masses, but instead a modern impression of complexity and scope.
(Brecht-Einzig, courtesy James Stirling)

indispensable to this effect. "Infinity," Burke said, "has a tendency to fill the mind with a delightful horror.")

In our own time, of course, great size no longer necessarily implies great weight. Stone blocks have been replaced by stone veneer and huge masses of load-bearing masonry by carefully calculated networks of cables. Yet size retains its force: we can be as awed by the required elaboration of lightweight members as by the required collection of heavy ones. The exposed steel frames of the George Washington Bridge's pylons are at least as impressive as they would be if faced with stone. (Cass Gilbert, architect of the Woolworth Building, designed masonry casings for the pylons, but, because of cost, they were never executed; most of us are happy now that they weren't.) The crystalline facets of the glazed roof of James Stirling's engineering library at Cambridge, the spiderweb cables holding in tension the tent

Vittorio Giorgini's unfinished experimental ferrocement structure in Liberty, New York: Another example of the drama of magnitude without mass. (Photograph: Vittorio Giorgini)

Buckminster Fuller's Climatron, St. Louis Botanical Garden: A prototypical modern structure of impressive size.

structures of Frei Otto, the bizarre mesh framework of Vittorio Giorgini's ferrocement experiments in upstate New York, the lightweight geodesic domes of Buckminster Fuller—these offer the modern drama of magnitude without mass.

The power of magnitude to engender our wonder and admiration has at least three obvious sources. One is the way in which the size of a building is related to that of the earth. Earth size, although a real phenomenon, is one not visible or clearly comprehended, yet that size governs our every action. From our first struggle to move about the earth's surface, we come to know, through gravity, the force of its size more intimately than we know any other aspect of nature. The relationship of different buildings' sizes to this enduring constant of earth size has an inescapable effect on the structure of those buildings, and it is a more complex and a more interesting effect than if a building twice as tall as another had to be simply twice as strong, or if a beam with twice the span of another had to be twice as deep.

The real effect, as first pointed out by Galileo and as made clear in more recent times in Sir D'Arcy Thompson's 1917 *On Growth and*

Form, a landmark of biological literature, is that similar structures of different dimensions require strengthening in proportion to the *squares* of those dimensions. Thompson explains:

> If a match stick be two inches, and a similar be six feet (or thirty-six times as long), the latter will sag under its own weight 1,300 times as much as the other. To counteract this tendency, as the size of an animal increases the limbs tend to become thicker and shorter and the whole skeleton bulkier and heavier; bones make up some 8 percent of the body of mouse or wren, 13 or 14 percent of goose or dog and 17 or 18 percent of the body of a man. Elephant and hippopotamus have grown clumsy as well as big; and the elk is of necessity less graceful than the gazelle.

So it is with building construction, and there is even a limit beyond which particular structures are impossible: if made larger, they would collapse under the strain of their own weight. Architect Myron Goldsmith of Skidmore, Owings & Merrill has applied this principle to different types of bridge structures, showing that each type has its limit and that beyond these limits the structural system must be changed. "The steel skeleton of multistory buildings," Goldsmith

Myron Goldsmith's graph of the strengths of different bridge structures: Each has a limiting size, just as living creatures do. (Courtesy Myron Goldsmith)

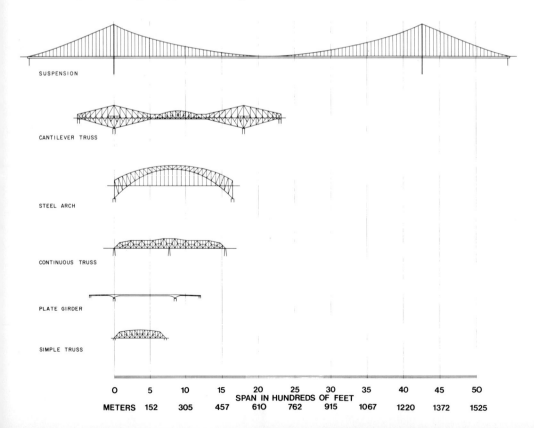

SUSPENSION

CANTILEVER TRUSS

STEEL ARCH

CONTINUOUS TRUSS

PLATE GIRDER

SIMPLE TRUSS

O	5	10	15	20	25	30	35	40	45	50

SPAN IN HUNDREDS OF FEET

| METERS | 152 | 305 | 457 | 610 | 762 | 915 | 1067 | 1220 | 1372 | 1525 |

has written, "exhibits a similar behavior. An eight-story building requires 10 pounds of steel per square foot, while a 100-story building
requires 30 pounds." Changes in building size thus demand changes
in building character.

A second source of the power of size to delight and impress us is
the relationship of buildings to our own bodies. The manipulation of
this relationship is one of architects' chief tools for controlling our
response to their work: Is a doorway secretive, beguiling, comfortable,
imposing, or triumphant? Its size, perceived in relationship to the
space our bodies actually need for walking through, is a major deter-
minant of its effect.

If not perceived correctly, of course, it will have an effect different
from the intended one. Frank Lloyd Wright, a master of size manipulation, fond of enhancing our appreciation of a large space by
squeezing us into it through a small one, wrote that

St. Peter's is invariably disappointing as a great building, for not until
the eye deliberately catches a human figure for purposes of comparison
with the building does one realize that the building is vast. Michelangelo
made the architectural details huge likewise, and the sense of grandeur
the whole might have had, were the great masses qualified by details that
were kept to human scale is lost. . . .

Yet, once St. Peter's size *is* realized, it affects our responses just
as we imagine Michelangelo intended. To quote again from Ruskin
(who didn't like the building very much either):

Disappointed as you may be, or at least ought to be, at first, by St. Peter's, in the end you will feel its size—and its brightness. These are all
you *can* feel in it—it is nothing more than the pump-room at Leamington
built bigger;—but the bigness tells at last: and Corinthian pillars whose
capitals alone are ten feet high, and their acanthus leaves three feet six
long, give you a serious conviction of the infallibility of the Pope, and the
fallibility of the wretched Corinthians, who invented the style indeed, but
built with capitals no bigger than hand-baskets.

But for most observers St. Peter's does more than suggest the Pope's
infallibility: As an invention of man it also suggests man's admirable
capability. The phenomenon that Wright described, the lack of a figure
we can use for comparison in judging the building's size, is one that
may be experienced from a distance—across the Tiber, for example,
or looking over the city from the Janiculum—but that disappears as
we near St. Peter's, for there is inevitably some familiar form at hand
for comparison. Except through photographs, which are notoriously
deceptive, we cannot approach a building without being there ourselves, and we know very well our own size.

The entrance of Santa Maria della Consolazione, Todi: The size of a practical door is contained within a small fraction of the size of the monumental door needed for an appropriate sense of importance. (Photograph: Stanley Abercrombie)

St. Peter's, Rome: Not until we notice the van in the courtyard do we fully realize the building's size. Seeing it in person, however, rather than in a photograph, we have available to us many such measuring aids. (Photograph: Fototeca Unione, Rome)

Mural in the Sala dei Giganti of Giulio Romano's Palazzo del Te, Mantua: Architecture is the art to which we entrust our lives. (Photograph: Alinari)

The fact that St. Peter's and many other vast structures can have a magnificent effect should puncture the curious notion that ideal buildings and building elements should be human in scale. It is fine if they often are adjusted precisely to the requirements of our body size, but to limit them to such size—to provide, for example, doorways no larger than we need for walking through—would be a destructive curtailment of the architect's vocabulary. The most exhilarating effects in architecture, in fact, are those that, relative to man, are quite excessive. In *Icon and Idea*, Sir Herbert Read wrote:

The greatness of Gothic was due to its superhumanity, to the free exploitation of abstract elements . . . without any purpose other than "the union of the individual with the universal". . . . Such an aim is not *in*human; on the contrary, it is the liberation of human faculties from the oppression of our personal, limited vision.

The Wellington Memorial, Dublin: Without any knowledge of construction techniques, we can appreciate the effort of building. (From *Joyce's Dublin*, Irish Heritage Series, No. 36)

Building size is related to our body size in another fundamental way. Because of its mass, however constructed or arranged, relative to the frailty of our bodies, architecture is a potential threat. At its best, sound and secure, it shelters and protects us; but at its worst, it can be fatal to its occupants. Architecture is the art to which we entrust our lives, and this act cannot help but produce in us some sense of a special kinship: the thrill of risk, the respect that accompanies willing subservience.

A third way in which building size impresses us has its origin both in the force of gravity and in the strength of man: Great buildings are not erected without great effort, and it is natural that we be respectful of an extraordinary expenditure of effort. It is not at all necessary to

Erecting the obelisk in front of St. Peter's, as seen in an etching from Carlo Fontana's *Templum Vaticanum:* It took 140 horses and more than 900 men to pull the 48 ropes that raised the ancient stone to a vertical position. (Courtesy American Academy in Rome)

have an understanding of historical construction techniques to realize something of the work required to assemble the stones of an observatory in the jungles of the Yucatán, or to build the dome of Santa Sophia, or to transport obelisks from Heliopolis to Rome and reerect them. This innate appreciation for the struggle of building is not diminished by the development of stronger and more sophisticated tools; the immediate need for manual labor may be reduced, but the labor-saving devices must still be engineered by means of mental labor, and they must be powered by energy resources that are valuable to man.

Building magnitude is not limited to the height or bulk of a single structure; it can refer, to no lesser degree, to the extensiveness of a number of small elements. A hall of a thousand columns can awe us in the same way and for the same reasons as a single giant tower, and repetition, despite its undeserved reputation for being boring, is one of the architect's key tools: Even the humblest form, presented with enough frequency, can produce a strong effect.

It must be clear as well that, powerful as it may be, the fact of size alone is not enough to earn our admiration for a building. Certainly a small building can be very fine (Brunelleschi's Pazzi Chapel and Bramante's even smaller Tempietto being two celebrated examples from the Renaissance). And at least two of the tallest buildings in the world, the twins of The World Trade Center in New York, fail, despite their size, to enter the ranks of impressive architecture; partly this failure results from the blatant inappropriateness of their delicate detailing to the buildings' potentially overpowering size. As if their own architect had tried to disguise the towers' size, they are dressed like elephants in tutus. As Ada Louise Huxtable wrote in the *New York Times*, they constitute "a conundrum: the daintiest big buildings in the world."

Conversely, we are aware of esthetic failure when a building pretends to be larger than we know it to be. Such pretense sometimes has a comic result, sometimes a pathetic one. In 1946, a time when traditional compositions, particularly in residential design, were being shrunk by economic constraints, Elizabeth B. Mock, author of *If You Want to Build a House*, warned against "shriveled copies" of mansions. "Grandeur reduced becomes absurdity," she advised, "and the Little King rarely cuts a regal figure."

Granting that size must be both correctly perceived and appropriately expressed, granting, too, that Ruskin is right in calling "mere weight . . . a clumsy way" of making an impression, it is nevertheless

Remains of the Brazen Palace, Anuradhapura, India: A hall of a thousand columns can impress us in the same way as a single giant tower. (Photograph: Frederico Borromeo)

Gas refinery, Ypsilanti, Michigan: Primary geometric forms sufficiently large to be exciting. (Photograph: Balthazar Korab)

An anti-tank defense line built during World War II: The multiplication of any form, no matter how banal when seen singly, and no matter what its use, can produce a powerful visual effect. (Photograph: Imperial War Museum, London)

true that size can impress. In relating dramatically to earth size, to body size, and to construction effort, the sheer bigness of buildings contributes to our delight in architecture. Yet, within any building size, what a myriad of shapes are possible! The design of those shapes is a more subtle and a much more complicated way of affecting our response to architecture.

The Shape of Architecture

Form is a mystery which eludes definition but makes man feel good in a way quite unlike social aid.

Alvar Aalto, lecture to the Architects' Association of Vienna, 1955

All objects within the range of our perception have shape. In every shape, even the most negligible, there is some small but real kernel of information for us and, therefore, some degree of potential pleasure available simply from the apprehension of the shape, for our minds delight in recognition, and there is a special satisfaction for us in those buildings or building elements that can be identified as discrete wholes. To borrow a term from philosophy, we seek and enjoy a *gestalt*, a dictionary definition of which is "a structure or configuration . . . so integrated as to constitute a functional unit with properties not derivable from its parts in summation." In addition to this basic satisfaction afforded by our perception of them, shapes arrest our attention, invite our curiosity, thrill us or repel us in the greatest possible variety of ways. Some, because they come laden with specific messages, affect us in ways that are easily understood, others in ways difficult to explain. With or without explanation, the power of shapes is indisputable.

Given sufficient size, the pyramid is one shape that exerts such power. Its effectiveness is enhanced, certainly, by its repetition through history and by the richness of its accumulated associations. For the Egyptians, who recognized it as a grandiose and idealized

The Roman Pantheon: Its great drum is a form that not only exhibits an exterior surface but also suggests something of its internal volume. (Photograph: Stanley Abercrombie)

transformation of the commonplace burial mound, who believed in it as a guarantee of a pharaoh's immortality, and who, seeing its gilt cap reflect the first direct rays of the rising sun, saw the image of divinity—for them, obviously, the pyramid had a significance that we can never recover for ourselves. Yet it moves us still. After all those who might recognize its origins and share the faith of its builders have vanished, the shape remains, and it remains powerful. It has a strength that is intrinsic.

The obelisk is another shape of fundamental appeal; it is difficult, though not impossible, to design an obelisk that will not capture our attention. It would be disingenuous to deny that the obelisk symbolizes the phallus, but it is wrong to see this association as the sole source of its striking appeal. That source may have less to do with sex than it does with a defiant gesture in the face of gravity, an exertion against inertia. We could even say that the sight of an erect phallus (or an outflung arm, or the elevated leg of a ballerina) owes some of its arresting effect to such structural exertion in contrast to the body's

Ricardo Bofill's pyramidal Parc de la Marca Hispanica at the French-Spanish border: Given sufficient size, the pyramid has indisputable power. (Serena Vergano, courtesy of Taller de Arquitectura)

Niched walls of white limestone at the entrance to Zoser's funerary complex, Sakkara, Egypt: Elemental shapes, but made forceful through size and repetition. (Photograph: Stanley Abercrombie)

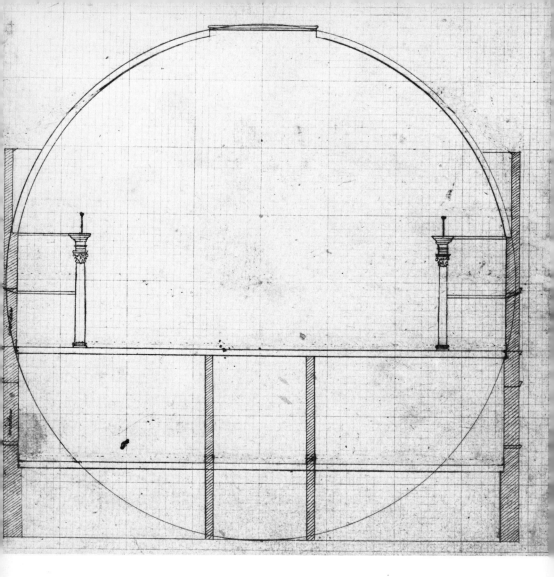

Thomas Jefferson's drawings for the Rotunda at the University of Virginia: Building form determined by geometry. (Photograph: Manuscripts Department, University of Virginia Library)

usual repose. Anyone, at least anyone since Freud, can see architecture as a symbol of sex; we should also be able to see sex as a symbol of construction.

The dome is another fundamental architectural shape that owes its strong appeal to something less simplistic than its analogy with the female breast. As with the obelisk, we marvel at its structural accomplishment. The dome, indeed, differs from the pyramid and the ob-

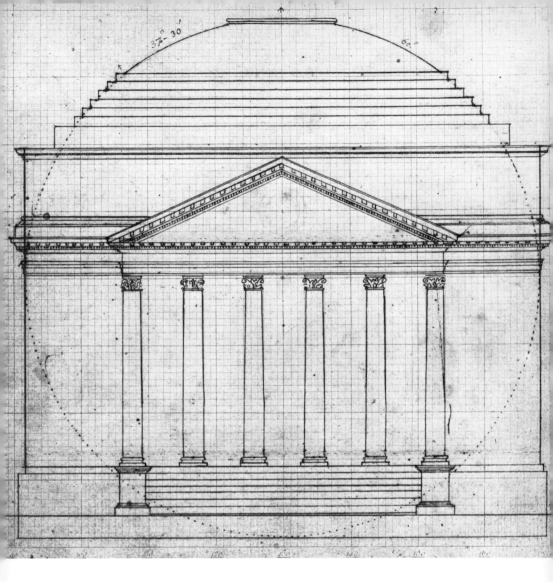

elisk, representing as it does a different class of shape, one beyond
the scope of sculpture and peculiar to architecture. We could call this
a building *form*, using the term to mean a shape that not only has an
external surface but that also suggests something of its internal space
and organization. We can say, in general, that form is superior to mere
shape, that architecture is at its most potent when exterior and interior
can be comprehended as one, when plan and volume are inseparably
united, when, in Le Corbusier's phrase, "the section is the elevation."
(Yet, admittedly, there are other cases in which an interior volume
of the most profoundly affecting shape lacks exterior identification.)

Inside or outside, it is often the most simple masses or volumes

41

Above, small stupa on the site of Sirkap, Taxila, West Pakistan; *right,* nave, St. Michael, Hildesheim, Germany: Inside or outside, it is often the most simple masses or volumes that appeal most strongly. (Photograph above: Frederico Borromeo; right photograph: Bildarchiv Foto Marburg)

Towers that guarded World War II German barracks near Angers, France: Some shapes fascinate us precisely because of their unfamiliarity. (Photograph: Imperial War Museum, London)

that appeal most strongly, but beyond these primary shapes of familiar potency lies a multitude of more esoteric possibilities: shapes, mandala-like, that evoke some emotional response from us, that fuel our imagination, that seem inexplicably to possess iconic strength. We may never have seen them before; they fascinate us precisely because of their unfamiliarity.

Shape may be reinforced or obscured by other shapes. Powerful as buildings of single shape may be, such buildings are rarities, for our functional programs generally require a complex combination of elements. This requirement is not necessarily an esthetic limitation; the architect can produce impressive effects by combining forms, by repeating the same form, or by surprising us with the juxtaposition of two quite disparate forms, provided that our initial surprise is followed by an acknowledgment that the disparities can be joined into a single composition.

Even when a single shape dominates, there is often a need for a different subsidiary shape and, skillfully manipulated, this sort of combination can also be welcome, the pinch of salt that enlivens the cookie batter. "All beautiful lines," Ruskin thought, "are mechanically drawn and organically transgressed," and Rhys Carpenter, in *The Esthetics of Greek Architecture,* wrote of forms "harmonized with mathematical precision and then irregularized." Following Le Corbusier, many of our best architects today are adept at contrasting a simple, straightforward major shape with a much more lyrical minor shape that could be said to have "organically transgressed" it.

And when a building composition consists of repeated elements, functional requirements often dictate differences. The vaults of Louis Kahn's Kimbell Art Museum in Fort Worth, for example, are not all the same length, and some, but not all, are interrupted to allow for interior courtyards, yet the unity of the whole is never in question. We have, in fact, a healthy tolerance for such variations.

Forms and shapes may also be either reinforced or obscured by surface treatment. Applied ornamentation has its undeniable values, and the architecture that denies itself these values is an impoverished one. The pleasures of ornament, however, are the pleasures of painting

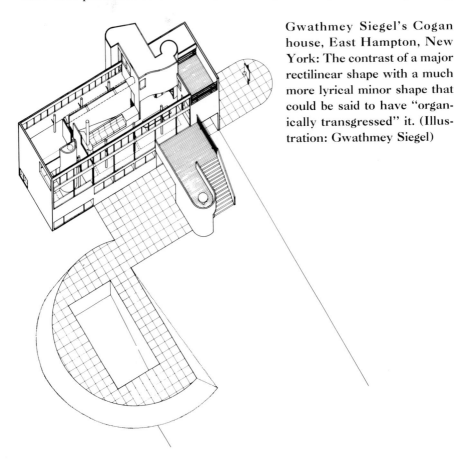

Gwathmey Siegel's Cogan house, East Hampton, New York: The contrast of a major rectilinear shape with a much more lyrical minor shape that could be said to have "organically transgressed" it. (Illustration: Gwathmey Siegel)

Louis Kahn's Kimbell Art Museum, Fort Worth: Although the parallel vaults are not all the same length and although some are interrupted by interior court-yards, the unity of the whole composition is unquestioned. (Bob Wharton, courtesy Kimbell Art Museum)

and sculpture; to find the pleasures of architecture, we must look not only at the surface but also at the substance beneath; it is there that we will discover what the nineteenth-century American sculptor, functionalist, and moralist Horatio Greenough called "the majesty of the essential."

This may be one reason that present taste prefers its Greek temples with their original coloration faded away: not because we dislike the colors or are offended by the ornamentation, but because, thus cleansed, the forms are more easily read. This is the reason, too, that a major share of our pleasure in architecture is not available from those

The Duomo, Lucca: We delight in the fact that each colonnette on the facade has its own pattern. (Photograph: Fototeca Unione, Rome)

The roof of the Palazzo Barberini, Palestrina: Tile patterns that elucidate the form beneath. (Photograph: Stanley Abercrombie)

buildings that depend solely on surface decoration while ignoring the shapes being decorated. As the neoclassical theorist Marc Antoine Laugier wrote in the middle of the eighteenth century, "Ornament squandered on a building lacking good proportions cannot succeed." And in *Form and Civilization,* the English writer, teacher, and practicing architect W. R. Lethaby must have had architecture specifically in mind when he warned that "Art is not a special sauce applied to ordinary cooking; it is the cooking itself if it is good."

But for the same reason, because ornament is superficial to shape, we can be quite relaxed about its consistency so long as the shape beneath is secure. We are not displeased—rather, we are delighted—when the great piers of Durham Cathedral or the colonnettes of the Duomo at Lucca are surfaced with different patterns, for the power of the whole composition, in each case, is so well established that these little variations cannot threaten it.

A building by Gino Coppedé in the Quartiere Dora, Rome: Ornament can be a pleasure in itself and can even bring architecture to life, but ornament never *is* architecture. (Photograph: Stanley Abercrombie)

48

There is even a sort of ornament that, paradoxically, helps us to see what it covers, ornament that arises as an informed consequence of building shape or construction. A pattern of roof tiles may demonstrate the slope or curve of the roof below; a stack of quoins may emphasize the turning of a corner; a molding may mark the juncture of two materials. These ornaments may be as decorative as any others, but they are also elucidations.

Many very interesting buildings, of course, have little to offer us *but* ornament, although some heavily ornamented ones offer much more. The perceptive English architect Peter Smithson, speaking about "the great baroque churches," pointed out that even they "are not at all theatrical in the expressionist . . . sense, but rather communicate their meaning primarily by space, and by absolute consistency of plastic language. And these tools," he added, "are still available—in fact are the *only* tools of architecture." Ornament, then, can be admirable in itself; in its relationship to the form beneath it, it can either obscure architecture or clarify it, either smother it or bring it to life. But ornament never *is* architecture.

The lack of ornament has its uses, too. The eighteenth-century architect Étienne-Louis Boullée thought plainness could convey an emotional state appropriate to funerary architecture:

> It does not seem possible to me to conceive anything sadder than a monument composed of a smooth, naked and unadorned surface . . . absolutely bare of details, and of which the decoration is formed by a composition of shadows, drawn by shadows still darker.

We can also find pleasure in a shape that is incomplete. We often admire that which is not immediately obvious, and the artist is wise to capitalize on such admiration. As Pater wrote of Michelangelo,

> In a way quite personal and peculiar to himself which often is, and always seems, the effect of accident, he secured for his work individuality and intensity of expression, while he avoided a too hard realism. . . . What time and accident [have done for other works] this effect Michelangelo gains by leaving nearly all his sculpture in a puzzling sort of incompleteness, which suggests rather than realizes actual form. . . . That incompleteness is Michelangelo's equivalent for colour in sculpture; it is his way of etherealizing pure form, of relieving its hard realism, and communicating to it breath, pulsation, the effect of life.

It is also his way of involving the observer as a participant in the discovery of form, in imagining the human body struggling to emerge from the stone. Similarly, architecture in a ruined state often charms us, inviting our imaginations to supply the missing lintels, to see whole

The Piazza Santa Cecilia, Rome, as it appeared earlier in this century: The "puzzling sort of incompleteness" of forms struggling to emerge. (Photograph: Fototeca Unione, Rome)

the broken columns, to erase the years of damage, to reconstruct its architect's intent, and—as with buildings of any age or condition—to imagine the life within it.

In ruins and new buildings alike, of course, there is no pleasure in a puzzle impossible to solve, and the architect, in employing the tools of formal variation, transgression, ornamentation, and incompleteness, must beware of their overuse and a consequent formal incoherence. It is no good to start with the exceptions and hope some whole will become discernible; a sense of the whole must be present from the start. We cannot devise a clever formal interruption before we have a form to interrupt, nor does sound architecture come from designing ornament first, then a scaffolding to support it. William Empson, in *Seven Types of Ambiguity*, wrote convincingly of the usefulness (for a writer) of those phrases that have multiple meanings, something par-

Fragments on the site of the Roman theater at Hierapolis: The intrigue of architectural forms in ruin. (Photograph, Fototeca Unione, Rome)

allel to what Charles Jencks seems to mean by "multivalence" in architecture, but Empson warned that the methods he had been describing "leave a poet in a difficult position. Even in prose the belief in them is liable to produce a sort of doctrinaire sluttishness; one is tempted to set down a muddle in the hope that it will convey the meaning more immediately." The same warning obviously applies to architecture.

But when they are not muddles, shapes in isolation have much to say to us. And when shapes are more than outlines, when they are eloquent about their own composition and about the spaces they contain—when they deserve the name *form*—their message is particularly rich.

The messages of shape sometimes have nothing to do with beauty; some of them are quite literal, didactic, or even hortatory. The shape chosen for the plan of a Christian church, for example, can be a cross, or it can be some less obvious Christian symbol such as a fish; it can be an equilateral triangle because the shape is understood to represent the Holy Trinity, or it can be a circle because that shape best shows, in Palladio's words, "the unity, infinite essence, uniformity and justice of God."

It must also be realized that, given some strong vision of the whole work, some foreknowledge of the desired formal destination, an architect has many ways to travel. Most of the decisions that must be made deal not with the whole but with its constituent parts. Here also the consideration of shape prevails, but what must be considered is not the impact of a shape in isolation, but the relationships of part to part and of parts to the whole. For only a few shapes are privileged to speak to us alone; most must speak together with others, with their masters and servants in an elaborate hierarchy within a single composition, or with neighboring shapes that are their equal counterparts. From their combined voices, their mutual influence, their harmony or discord, derives much of the character of any work of architecture.

The Shapes within Architecture

One may regard a work of architecture as a living organism in which all parts of its aspect . . . must follow the same rhythm, for lacking this it runs a great risk of not being able to thrive.

André Lurçat, *Architecture*

Shapes can work together to produce compositional coherence by means of similarity, repetition, or proportion. Similar shapes need not be exactly similar, of course, for us to recognize a rapport between them; a family resemblance is enough and sometimes, because of the pleasure of variety, even preferable to perfect congruence. It is not possible to imagine any shape for which there is not some possible complement, for the principle of unity through similarity holds happily together even those shapes that are, in isolation, highly idiosyncratic, verbally indescribable, or downright ugly.

The much-maligned L-shape, for example, often avoided because of its awkward lack of a dominant directional gesture, can come into its own in the presence of other L-shapes, all interlocked into an intriguing whole. And a concave curve or a convex one can often be seen at its best in the company of other curves, preferably—for architecture is preeminently three-dimensional—in different planes and configurations, a curve in the building plan preparing us for a curve in the facade or for a vaulted ceiling or even a dome. Any shape, in fact, if effectively recalled, echoed, mirrored, or somehow referred to by other shapes, can be the basis for a sound design.

A window of the Pretura, Capua: Sympathetic but not necessarily identical forms. (Photograph: Fototeca Unione, Rome)

A detail of the facade, Santa Maria della Pace, Rome: A curve in one plane prepares us for a complementary curve in another. (Photograph: Stanley Abercrombie)

Similarity of shape, of size, or of character can be critical in binding different parts of a building into a successful composition. The American journal *Architectural Review*, writing in 1899 about Richard Morris Hunt's Fifth Avenue front for the Metropolitan Museum of Art, said that

. . . this design possesses real distinction; it has the grand air, it is monumental and dignified. But it sins in one important respect: there is no common measure of scale for the wings and the central mass. Every detail of the latter is colossal; every detail of the wings is small and fine, so that instead of harmonizing, like parts of one whole, the bigness of one and the littleness of the other are both exaggerated to their mutual disadvantage.

When a shape is joined by others that are not merely similar but are exact duplicates, we have the special case of a composition that can be said to be modular, and modularity has particular virtues of its own. There are virtues of construction practicality, obviously, there being efficiency in the use of concrete blocks all of the same size or of plywood panels all the same. The modular approach to the craft

Richard Morris Hunt's Fifth Avenue front for the Metropolitan Museum of Art, New York: "No common measure of scale for the wings and the central mass." (Photograph: AIA Foundation Prints and Drawings Collection)

of building does not have as its primary aim the accomplishment of art but simply the accomplishment of orderly construction. Using as a module some unit such as ten centimeters (which is, conveniently, almost exactly the same as four inches), it may seek to promulgate that module's use by manufacturers of various building materials. The greatest part of an architect's time and effort in detailing a building is spent on the joining of different materials; if all those materials— bricks, tile, refrigerators, door bucks, shower stalls—were dimensioned in multiples of ten centimeters, how much easier the architect's work could be, and how much neater the results!

Even without the use of such standardized components, there is a satisfying sense of parsimony about the use of identical structural bays—as in a Gothic cathedral, for example, with repeated pier sizes

James Stirling's dormitories for St. Andrews University: Built with a large number of identical precast concrete panels, the evident modularity of the result offers a high degree of visual order. (Photograph above: Brecht-Einzig, courtesy James Stirling; photograph opposite: James Stirling)

A three-dimensional number grid developed by architect Ezra Ehrenkrantz for the British Research Station displays numbers that, if used exclusively for the dimensions of building materials, produce modular construction. (Photograph: Stanley Abercrombie)

and repeated rib patterns—rather than having each bay be an independent invention. Such a modular relationship of shapes is different from the others discussed here in three ways: it deals less directly with esthetics; even though it has two-dimensional and three-dimensional effects, it may be concerned primarily with the repetition of a one-dimensional size; and it is perfectly sensible. Yet even this commonsense matter of efficiency through modularity has, because of the fact—the important fact—that esthetic success is often aided by orderliness, some beneficial esthetic side effects, some of which have been elaborated into near-poetry and related to many other fields by

The so-called Baker's Monument at the Porta Maggiore, Rome: A stunning visual presence due to the repeated circular holes. The alleged significance of the holes—that they represent ancient Roman ovens—is interesting additional information, but not necessary for the visual effect. (Photograph: Stanley Abercrombie)

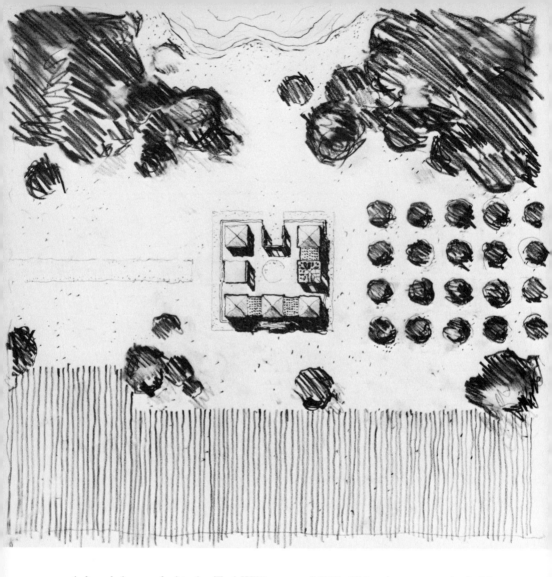

A beach house design by Tod Williams and Billie Tsien is composed of eight separate building elements, all identical in size and similar in shape. (Illustration: Tod Williams)

Buckminster Fuller (in his own words "a comprehensivist in an era of almost total specialization").

And modularity offers some purely esthetic virtues, too, for it invites us to a particularly easy game of seeking relationships between units, of matching and multiplying, of seeing common joints and shared alignments. The traditional Japanese house, irregular as its outline may be, exudes a sense of serenity, poise, and coherence that has

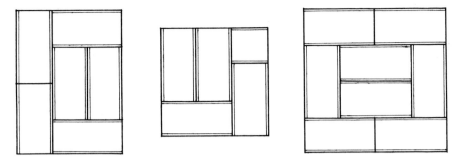

Plans for traditional Japanese rooms in 6-, 4½-, and 8-*tatami* sizes.

much of its basis in the modularity of its plan: a cluster of rooms each of which is sized to exactly accommodate a number of *tatami* mats, each mat being identical in size (about three feet by six, although, traditionally, the size varied slightly from province to province) and in shape (a double square).

Special even among modular compositions are those in which the module is a square, its length repeated in every unit to the exclusion of all other lengths, lacking directional emphasis, and sharing even more alignments. Without some variation, however, the visual game provided by a square module can be *too* easy to play. Note how William Kessler, in his Coleman Young Recreation Center, Detroit, makes the game interesting by juggling a whole array of square grids, ranging from four-inch-square tiles to four-foot-square ceiling grids that shield mechanical equipment from view; or see how Arata Isozaki's museum in Gunma prefecture, Japan, while based on a compositional diagram assembled entirely of cubes, is infinitely more varied and interesting than the diagram. The search for compositional coherence through the use of similar or repeated shapes offers many opportunities for variety and complexity.

But more complex and subject to more arcane analysis is the use of proportion; here we have lengths and shapes that are not related by means of obvious similarity, but by the dictates of abstract systems. In Egypt, in Greece, in Renaissance Italy, and in our own century— indeed, in many of the most well-developed phases of the history of architecture—attention has been paid to the related notions that systems of proportion will offer helpful guides to artful building, that architects with command of such systems will be better equipped than those without them, and that users of architecture will somehow perceive systematically proportioned buildings as being superior. Gen-

William Kessler's Coleman Young Recreation Center, Detroit: The game of juggling an array of square grids in varied sizes. (Photograph: William Kessler)

Arata Isozaki's museum in Gunma prefecture, Japan: While based on a compositional diagram assembled entirely of cubes, the finished building is infinitely more varied and interesting than the diagram. (Photograph: Masao Arai, courtesy The Japan Architect Co., Ltd.; illustration: Arata Isozaki)

Another Isozaki design, the Fukuoka Mutual Bank in Nagasumi, is based more rigidly on the manipulation of a square grid. (Taisuke Ogawa, courtesy The Japan Architect Co., Ltd.)

erally, systems of proportion have not been proposed because of any proof of their beautiful results but because of some other real or imagined properties. These properties are various, but most of them fall within one or a combination of four categories: those concerned with music, age, nature, and arithmetic.

One of the most durable categories of proportioning systems is of those proposed because of their musical analogies. Proponents of such systems have observed the simple mathematical relationships in the lengths of strings and the lengths of vibrating air columns in musical instruments, relationships that combine to produce pitch, and they have taken a long leap to the conclusion that such relationships must look as harmonious as they sound. Architect and theorist Leone Battista Alberti, for example, writing in 1485, advised that ". . . numbers by means of which the agreement of sound affects our ears with delight are the very same which please our eyes and our minds." If that were true, *why* would it be true? Geronimo Cardano, a sixteenth-century Italian philosopher, physician, and mathematician, suggested one possible reason: "In hearing, the known is called consonance; in seeing, beauty. . . . For there is delight in knowing, as there is sadness in not knowing." And the Franciscan monk Francesco di Giorgi went so far as to interpret interplanetary distances in terms of musical tones (in *De harmonia mundi*, Venice, 1525) and was then invited by Doge Andrea Gritti to apply his theories to Jacopo Sansovino's design for the church of San Francesco della Vigna. (According to the late Rudolf Wittkower, the consummate historian of proportion theory, Giorgi expressed the proportions between his suggested nave dimensions in terms of octaves and fifths.) Harmony, whether concerned with music, with the planets, or with architecture, is seen to result from the use of numbers that relate to each other in simple, therefore easily known, ratios.

Understandable commensurability does seem to be a source of architectural harmony; it is reasonable to suppose that the eye finds satisfaction in discerning mathematical relationships between building elements, and that only the very simplest of mathematical relationships are so discernible. But the same understanding is not a source of musical harmony. As Pythagoras discovered, strings in the ratio of 3 to 2 units of length, bowed or plucked together, do produce the musical interval called a fifth; strings in the ratio of 2 to 1 produce an octave; the fifth and the octave are pleasant sounds. However, they are not pleasant because our ears detect in them the relationships 3 to 2 or 2 to 1. When we hear a fifth, we may be able to hear the two separate notes that have combined to produce it, but it is impossible to hear

The church of St. George, near Novgorod, Russia: Unity through the repeated use of similar shapes. (Photograph: William Brumfield)

the mathematical relationships between those two notes. Nor does our anatomy encourage looking for aural-visual parallels: the German physicist and biologist von Helmholtz, over a century ago, established that our perceptions of musical harmony are related to the vibrations of membranes in our ears, membranes that have little in common with the tissues of our retinas and optic nerves.

The difference between aural and visual harmony is also shown by the concept of dissonance. In music, a slight variation in the tuning of a perfect interval can produce an impression of dissonance. In architecture, when we see a group of otherwise equal rectangles—a row of granite panels, for example—the presence of one slightly smaller rectangle in the group can produce a similar unpleasant sensation.

Side elevation, Gwathmey Siegel's Weitz beach house, Quogue, New York: A carefully calculated composition of similar rectangles at different sizes and in different relationships to each other. (Norman McGrath, courtesy Gwathmey Siegel)

Facade of the Palace of Basamtapur, Katmandu: An equally careful but very different composition of more esoteric shapes. (Photograph: Giraudon, Paris)

When we see a single rectangle in isolation, however, it can never look dissonant. Even assuming the possible existence of a perfectly proportioned rectangle, a slight variation from that perfection will satisfy us just as well.

The value of music as a model for an absolute standard is further weakened by the fact that the dissonance or consonance of musical notes is not a permanent condition, but varies in accordance with both historical and musical context. What the Greeks determined to be perfect tuning is not what we hear in the tuning of a present-day piano, and a chord that would seem dissonant in a Brahms quartet could sound perfectly correct in a composition by Stockhausen.

"Music and architecture are alike a matter of measure," as Le Corbusier maintained, but they are matters measured in two very different ways, and both systems of measurement are variable. The two arts are genuinely related only in the sense that they share a quality of being apprehended incrementally, music in increments of time, architecture in increments of space (and in the time needed to move through space.) They can each also be made to stand as metaphor for the other, a common conceit because of music's envy of architecture's permanence and architecture's envy of music's abstraction. But to search the mechanics of musical harmony for justification of a system of architectural proportions is an effort that cannot succeed.

A second category of proportioning systems purports to disclose the secrets of the ancients. The Egyptian pyramids and the Parthenon have been the most frequent victims of efforts to establish the ancient use of proportion. Scale models of the Great Pyramid of Cheops, constructed in plastic but with exactly authentic proportions, have been credited with astonishing properties such as keeping ground beef fresh for months and sharpening used razor blades, and the number of curves and diagonal lines projected on drawings of the Parthenon's west front would, placed end to end, stretch from here to stupefaction. The ground beef mystery seems outside the scope of this book, however, and, so far, none of the Parthenon overlays has conclusively shown the system the Greek architects must have used. (It seems never to have been undertaken, by the way, to disprove the proposition that beautiful rectangles, squares, and circles can also be superimposed on some of the ugliest facades ever built.)

An early example of the alleged disclosure of ancient secrets was the recording, by the Roman author and architect Vitruvius, of an elaborate series of Greek proportioning rules. (For just one example: "The thickness of the frame in front is to be equal to one-twelfth the height of the door, and is to diminish towards the top a fourteenth part of its width.") Like the lines projected on the Parthenon, however, attempts to show that the whole set of Vitruvian rules is based on a single simple proportioning system, from which other rules can be derived, have been unconvincing.

Even if these attempts had been persuasive, the ancients' knowledge can be granted superiority over current knowledge only if the ancients' buildings can be accepted as superior, and such is not consistently the case. Some buildings of the ancient world are undeniable masterpieces, but not all, and if the creation of masterpieces were "made easy" by a set of rules, why weren't the rules used more often? The use of age alone as the justification for any system of proportions must be viewed with suspicion.

A third category, that concerned with nature, claims value for whatever systems of proportion can be detected in such natural wonders as the intersecting curves on the head of the sunflower or the geometry of a snow crystal. Nature, in this view and in the words of Alberti, "is the best and divine teacher of all things."

Here again, there are difficulties. While it may be impossible to imagine an ugly snow crystal, it is easy to imagine that a building that looked like a snow crystal might be ridiculous. It is only fair to admit that advocates of the nature category of proportion theory never say that buildings should look like crystals, but only that they should use the design principles discerned in such natural forms as crystals. Even so, such a prescription must be based on the assumption that the principles structuring nature inevitably produce beautiful results. We know this to be false: The Arctic Circle, full of snow crystals, is reported to be bleak, the Gila monster is unattractive, and there are even sunsets with disgusting color combinations. Naturalists rightly find every aspect of nature worthy of study and of some degree of conservation, but all nature cannot be called beautiful.

One subcategory of the nature school deserves more serious attention, however: the search for a system of proportion in man himself. Just as the Gila monster is presumably beautiful in the eyes of other Gila monsters, so man (at least, an ideal man) is beautiful to mankind, the users of architecture. Further, the very use of architecture entails direct contact between buildings and bodies; the width of stair treads, the height of doorknobs, the length of bathtubs, and a thousand other dimensional aspects of a building necessarily relate to the dimensions of man. Coziness and spaciousness are sensations arising directly from the relationship of room size to body size.

Vitruvius suggested that the Greek orders were designed to correspond to different physical types—the Doric to a chunky male, the Ionic to a slender female. This may have been merely speculation, however, and it may have been Vitruvius himself who first looked seriously at man's body as a source of architectural proportion. He observed that a man—again, an ideal one—with legs apart and arms extended would touch the imaginary edges of two basic geometric figures, a square and a circle. It was a potent vision that was interpreted again and again, in slightly different ways, by different illustrators of Vitruvius's text. Wittkower wrote that "this simple picture seemed to reveal a deep and fundamental truth about man and the world, and its importance for Renaissance architects can hardly be overestimated. The image haunted their imagination." As an example, Wittkower quoted from the *Divina proportione* of Leonardo's friend Luca Pacioli: "First we shall talk of the proportions of man, because from the human

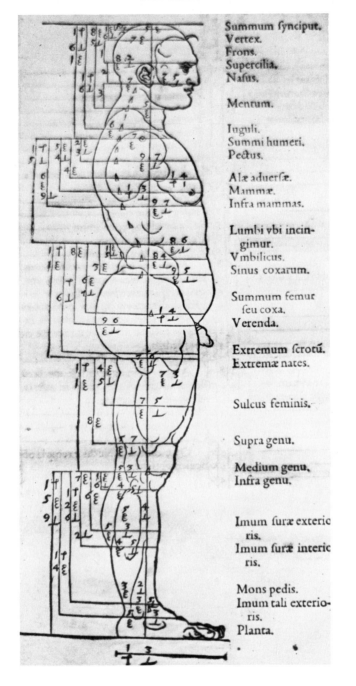

Summum ſynciput.
Vertex.
Frons.
Supercilia.
Naſus.

Mentum.

Iuguli.
Summi humeri.
Pectus.

Alæ aduerſæ.
Mammæ.
Infra mammas.

Lumbi vbi incin-
 gimur.
Vmbilicus.
Sinus coxarum.

Summum femur
 ſeu coxa.
Verenda.

Extremum ſcrotú.
Extremæ nates.

Sulcus feminis.

Supra genu.

Medium genu.
Infra genu.

Imum ſuræ exterio
 ris.
Imum ſuræ interio
 ris.

Mons pedis.
Imum tali exterio-
 ris.
Planta.

From Albrecht Dürer's *de Symmetria:* A search for mathematically exact relationships between parts of the human body. (Courtesy American Academy
in Rome)

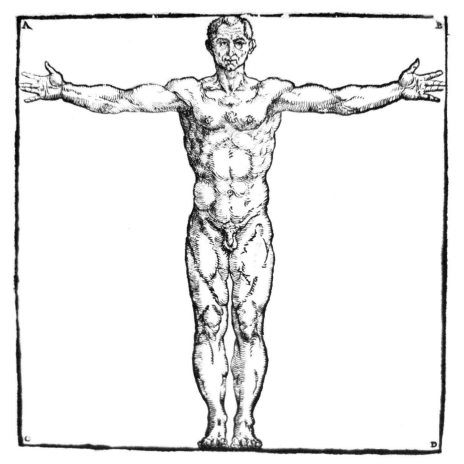

Vitruvian figures, in the version drawn by Giovanni Rusconi and published in 1590, extend their arms and legs to touch the edges of two essential shapes: the square and the circle. "This simple picture," Rudolf Wittkower wrote, "seemed to reveal a deep and fundamental truth about man and the world." (Courtesy American Academy in Rome)

body derive all measures and their denominations, and in it is to be found all and every ratio and proportion by which God reveals the innermost secrets of nature."

Pacioli was expressing both a simple fact and a rather fanciful theological speculation. The simple fact (at least it was a fact when he wrote it) that "from the human body derive all measures and their denominations" is obvious. Since they began to measure, people have found parts of their bodies handy for rough dimensioning. As long as the United States lags in conversion to the metric system, the foot

still survives as a measurement, and many older times and places, inhabited by people with similar foot sizes, have used the same measure. (The meter—one ten-millionth of the distance from the earth's equator to the pole, measured along a meridian—is, in comparison, abstract and arbitrary, however efficient.) Other units with anatomical origins have been the hand, the palm, and the digit. Their origins give these units no esthetic significance, of course.

Pacioli's speculation, however, that the human body is God's medium for expressing nature's "innermost secrets" does imply esthetic significance and was of compelling interest at the time it was written; today it is hardly supportable, hardly even understandable, and certainly not demonstrable. It cannot be shown, in fact, that any generally nature-based or specifically man-based system of proportion will necessarily lead us to better architecture. But we can say simply that architecture is so intimately related to man's body that no good building can neglect the relationship.

Some speculations about proportion have, of course, combined the rationalization of age with the rationalization of appearance in nature. That excellent architect Sir John Soane, for example, lecturing to the Royal Academy in the early nineteenth century, suggested that "the young student study incessantly . . . such harmony, fitness and mutal relation of parts as is found in the great productions of Nature, and experienced in the magical effect produced by the sublime Works of the Ancients." And Claude Perrault, architect of the Louvre's east facade, thought that "it was not without reason that the ancients thought those proportions which make the beauty of buildings were taken from the proportions of human bodies . . ." Perrault then observed that there is no single "ideal" figure, and he made use of this observation by suggesting that different figures might be the ideal models for different buildings; that is, as men fit for heavy labor are bulkier than those fit for polite discourse, a factory structure should be proportioned in accordance with a laborer's measurements, a concert hall with the measurements of a violinist. A nice conceit, but one that can hardly be recommended as standard policy in the drafting room.

Last, and really inseparable from the other three categories, is the group of proportioning systems that find justification in their own arithmetic. Because the relationships between numbers are lasting ones, the justification of arithmetic has about it some of the aura of the justification of age. As Paul T.Frankel wrote in *Form and Reform*, "Arithmetic and geometry exist independent of Time. Such beauty as their creations possess is innate and changeless," and Edna St. Vincent Millay claimed that "Euclid alone has looked on Beauty bare." The justification of arithmetic is also often combined with the justification of nature. Galileo, for example: "The great book of nature . . . is written in the language of mathematics."

To take the simplest possible case of arithmetic, the relationship of one to two can be considered valuable as a proportioning tool, not because it is analogous to the musical octave, but because of the very everyday facts that one times two equals two (offering a useful progression of related units: 1, 2, 4, 8, etc.) and that one plus one equals two (offering another useful progression : 1, 2, 3, 4, etc.). The geometric application of this childish arithmetic would give us two shapes that might be assumed to be—and are empirically known to be— visually satisfying: the square and the double square. It hardly gives

Santa Maria della Consolazione, Todi: an assemblage of primary geometric solids: cubes, rectangular solids, cylinders, and hemispheres. (Photograph: Stanley Abercrombie)

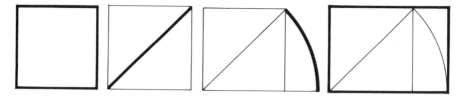

Left to right: a square, a diagonal through the square; the diagonal rotated; the resultant rectangle, its sides in the proportion of 1 to $\sqrt{2}$.

us more than those two shapes, for a rectangle with a length three or four times its height is perceived by us just as a long rectangle, not as a triple square or a quadruple square.

Other arithmetical systems are more complex and more interesting. Two of them are of particular importance in the theory of proportions, and both of them employ the use of irrational numbers. This fact alone, the fact that they depend upon the use of numbers that can never be expressed exactly, no matter to how many decimal places we may carry them, might seem to make them inappropriate for use in architecture, but that is not the case. Such is the roughness of our visual perception that the substitution of a whole number that is close to an irrational one will almost never be perceptible.

The first of the two important proportioning systems begins with a square and a diagonal drawn between its opposite corners. With one of its ends as the center, the diagonal is rotated, producing an arc, and the projection of one of the square's sides until it intersects that arc establishes a rectangle. A simple law of plane geometry tells us that the diagonal of our square is equal to the square root of the sum of two of the square's sides; the proportion of our rectangle is therefore one to the square root of two, and the sum of its sides is one plus the square root of two, or approximately 2.414. Although no whole number will ever give us the *exact* numerical equivalents of $\sqrt{2}$ or of $1 + \sqrt{2}$, there is a progression of whole numbers that approximates $1 + \sqrt{2}$. If we begin with the number one and move to the next higher number that, divided by one, most closely approximates 2.414, we move, obviously, to two. From two we move to five (5 divided by 2 being 2.5), from 5 to 12 (12 divided by 5 being 2.416), and so forth, so that the series of whole number approximations that, after some initial ups and downs, comes ever and ever closer to 2.414, is this: 1, 2, 5, 12, 29, 70, 169, etc. Now it happens that this progression, which is called Pell's series, has a curious characteristic: Every number in it, if doubled and added to its preceding number, equals its following number.

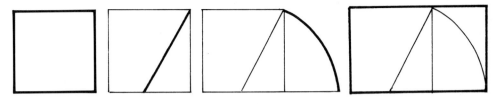

Left to right: a square; a line from one side's center to an opposite corner; the line rotated; the resultant "golden" rectangle, its sides in the proportion of 2 to $1 + \sqrt{5}$.

This characteristic may be interesting, but it has no esthetic implications for the rectangle associated with it. Nevertheless, a rectangle proportioned with the ratio of $1 + \sqrt{2}$, lying in that familiar range of rectangles between a square and a double square, is generally thought to be quite pleasant in shape. In addition, it has the virtue of being easily constructed on any building site, despite the irrationality of $\sqrt{2}$, by using a string as the rotating diagonal. When whole numbers must be used (and irrational numbers look pretty silly on architects' working drawings), approximations such as those in Pell's series are convenient substitutes.

At last we come to the most famous proportioning system of all, the system incorporated in Le Corbusier's "Modulor" and based on what have come to be called the "golden" rectangles and the "golden section." Beginning again with a square, this time we draw a diagonal from the center of one side to an opposite corner. Again we rotate the diagonal, forming an arc and then a rectangle. A rather nicely proportioned rectangle, we see, but its fame is based not so much on its pleasing shape (although that has adamantly been claimed for it) as on the following unusual properties:

The rectangle we have made has the proportion of 2 to $1 + \sqrt{5}$. If we remove from one end of it a square (for example, the square we started with), the remaining rectangle will *also* have the proportion of 2 to $1 + \sqrt{5}$. Remove another square, another similar rectangle

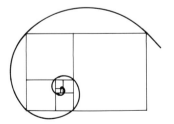

A logarithmic spiral connects the corners of a succession of squares and "golden" rectangles.

Detail of William Strickland's Merchant's Exchange Building, Philadelphia:
The spiral is a favorite motif in architecture. (Photograph: Julie Jensen)

remains, and so on, indefinitely. A further curiosity is that a simple
geometric figure—a spiral—will connect the corners of every square
in this endless progression of squares and rectangles, and the spiral,
of course, is reputed to be a favorite shape in nature, determining
the character of sunflower heads, snail shells, and spiral nebulae,
among other things. Presented literally, rather than as a proportioning
device, it is also a favorite motif in classical architecture, a fact that
suggests the transferability of its appeal from nature to art.

The numbers involved in this system are, again, irrational ones.
Some writers on the subject, such as Jay Hambridge, have seen a
virtue in this fact: The 2 to $1 + \sqrt{5}$ rectangle Hambridge calls "the
rectangle of the whirling squares," and the system of proportion based
upon it he calls "dynamic symmetry," its dynamic quality deriving
in some unexplained way from the fact that only an infinite number
of decimal places can define its numbers. Systems of proportion that
use whole numbers are "static" and, in Hambridge's opinion, "There
is no question of the superiority of the dynamic over the static."

Whether or not we accept this opinion, there is another progression

Roger C. Ferri's design for a pedestrian city: Built areas are shown hatched; the serpentine park system is dotted. As Ferri describes his project, "The streets, all of which are pedestrian, are formed by intersecting patterns of Fibonacci spirals. The curved paths provide perspectives that constantly unfold before the pedestrian as [the city] closes behind him. [The plan] offers a rhythmic revelation with each step. This provides a much richer urban drama than the axial path, whose vista is fully perceived at once, thus dissipating the initiative of discovery." (Illustration: Roger C. Ferri)

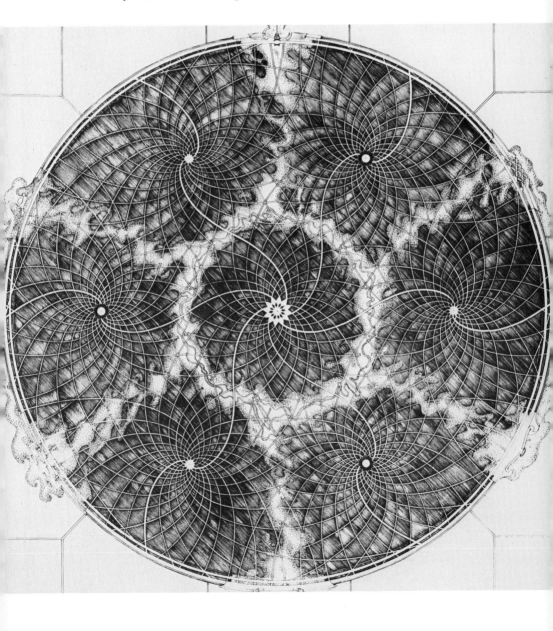

of whole, "static" numbers—this one called the Fibonacci series—
that approximates the ratio of one side of a "golden" rectangle to
another. This ratio, left in "dynamic"terms, is $1 + \sqrt{5}$ divided by
2, or approximately 1.618. Beginning again with one and moving at
each step to the next larger number that, divided by its precedent,
will give the result closest to 1.618, we obtain this series: 1, 2, 3, 5,
8, 13, 21, etc. Like Pell's series, the Fibonacci series has an intriguing
characteristic: In this case, every number in it, added to its preceding
number, equals the following number.

Understandably, many find such arithmetical coincidences entertaining. Admittedly, too, the ease of on-site construction of "golden"
rectangles (again, a string for swinging the arc is the only tool needed)
makes their use by the ancients quite believable. Their kinship to
the spiral structures of natural phenomena is also interesting. But there
is nothing inherent in any of this that promises architectural excellence.

Le Corbusier hedged his bet and complicated his own version of
the system by combining the arithmetic-as-magic rationalization with
the man-as-the-measure one. His Modulor system was based firmly
on the numbers of the Fibonacci series, but he also claimed that "some
of these values of measures can be described as being characteristically
related to the human stature." His diagrams show a figure with one
arm stretched above his head, and with several key points—his navel,
the top of his head, the tips of his raised fingers—corresponding to
dimensions on an accompanying scale. On the surface, this seems a
modern version of the Vitruvian figure touching the edges of its imaginary square and circle, but Le Corbusier was clear about his figure's
being different. Lecturing to the Architectural Association, London,
1947, he said: "One cannot accept the idea that is current and imagine
a man placed in the middle of a circle with simultaneous synthetic
perception." Drawing a diagrammatic Vitruvian figure, he said, "I
write above the circle 'high renaissance,' and underneath, 'it is false.'
Man has his eyes in front of him, not behind, and it is thus that he
gains his impression of architecture. It is pure illusion , this idea that
man can see from one side to another at the same time. The impression
of architecture is consecutive." Even so, whether in a circle or in a
"golden" rectangle, the human body was again being invoked in support of a system that—to let Le Corbusier continue—"is mathematics,
it is rich, it opens the door to miracles, the miracle of numbers."

If such miracles remain a matter of faith, does it follow that, for
disbelievers, proportion has no effective part in the production of architectural excellence? Certainly not. What is in doubt is only that

Entrance hall, Louis Kahn's Yale Center for British Art, New Haven: Here we can enjoy both the visual delights of well-considered proportions and the quiet order that comes from simple repetition. (Photograph: George Cserna)

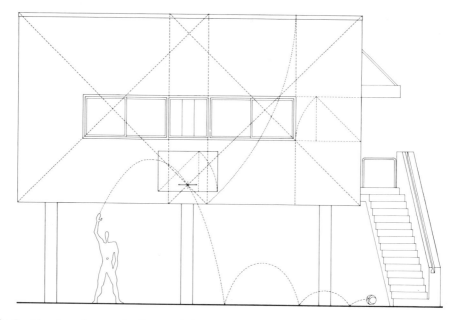

In his elevation study for an Atlanta studio, architect Anthony Ames shows
Le Corbusier's "Modulor" figure shooting baskets beneath an array of 1 to
√2 rectangles. (Illustration: Anthony Ames)

proportioning systems are effective because of any musical or natural
analogy, because of their age, or because of their arithmetic.

It is a shame that proponents of proportioning systems have so often
exaggerated their claims that the whole subject has been made suspect,
for there is a genuine and fundamental justification for such systems'
use: that the use of a proportioning system—*any* proportioning system—can give to a building an orderly relationship between its parts
that, even if only dimly perceived, is visually satisfying. This is the
real value of proportion and its only value. There is no magic about
it except the magic of man's reaction to orderliness. The superiority
of one system over another is so difficult to confirm that we may say
it hardly matters which system is used, so long as it is one that allows
a reasonable amount of variety and yet remains comprehensible. Along
with the simpler ordering techniques of shape similarity and modularity, the use of *some* system of proportion is one of the architect's
key tools.

Not that its usefulness is unlimited. Frank Lloyd Wright in *On Architecture* said that "Proportion is nothing in itself. It is a matter of
relation to environment, modified always by every feature, exterior

as well as interior." This is, obviously, an example of Wrightian hyperbole, for proportion *is* something of real value in itself; nevertheless, Wright, in this statement and also in his buildings, had a grasp of the important truth that local circumstance and character, as well as specific functional features, modify that value, and what may be the right proportion for a Chicago street may be quite wrong—no matter what the mathematics say—for a Wisconsin hillside.

Placement

One cannot overemphasize the fact that everything—meaning and value as well as appropriateness of individual human conduct or the energy state of an atom—depends upon the interaction of the thing itself and its environment.

Cyril Stanley Smith, "Structural Hierarchy in Science, Art, and History," in *On Aesthetics in Science*, Judith Wechsler, editor

Architecture never exists in a vacuum; it is touched on all sides by its context. Before it can even be created, the idea of its possibility has had to depend upon a social context both complex and crucial: It has had to come to terms with prevailing zoning ordinances and building codes, the current availability of trades and the current market for rentable space, the general economy of the community and the personal economy of the client. Once a suitable fit has been found with these determinants, then it becomes possible for an architect to consider the fit between the building and its physical surroundings; this is the beginning of architecture as art.

At its worst, architecture fits its site as a foreign, superfluous, or inappropriate addition. At its most innocuous, it slips into its context without disturbance. At its best, it is a concretization of place, a new reality that gathers and brings to a visible focus all the threads that, woven together, constitute the local reality. Some of these threads are physical, some abstract; they include the earlier structures, the passages between structures, the trees, shrubs, insects, view, fog, smell, temperature, names, and memories of the place—threads that,

A grotto in the park at Caserta, Italy: Landscape elements can take on the strength and importance of habitable structures. (Photograph: Fototeca Unione, Rome)

Left, the Church of the Redeemer, Lalibala, Ethiopia; *above*, the mouth of the rock sanctuary, Kondane, India: Structures carved from the surrounding rock have a rare intimacy with their surroundings. (Left photograph: Christopher H. L. Owen; photograph above: R. K. Sehgal, courtesy Archaeological Survey of India)

before the building's construction, might have been apprehended only vaguely.

One fundamental way in which a building can do such thread-gathering is by making a wise fit with the land. There are, obviously, many ways such a fit can be made (and they do not all, by any means, depend upon subservience of the new building to what came before it). The most intimate type of fit arises from a building technique little used today, the technique of creating architecture by carving out materials rather than by adding them together. Such structures, hewn from the rock in Ethiopia, Turkey, Jordan, India, and elsewhere, achieve a homogeneity with their context that is impossible in more conventional construction. The designed erosion of the mountain makes us more aware than before of the mountain's monolithic integrity.

Carved architecture, of course, is an exception. Most buildings are assembled on the ground, and their relationship to the ground is often their most distinctive aspect: They can rise straight from the soil, be stepped or terraced gradually, or be elevated on platforms or *piloti*. A complication almost always necessary for the architect to consider is that the building starts visually at grade but must start physically below grade, its walls continuing out of sight to footings buried below the frost line. It is not this footing condition but the critical junction of wall and ground surface that affects esthetic quality.

In the case of both building techniques—the rare technique of carving out and the common technique of building up—there can be a great drama in the juxtaposition of natural and built form. This drama is often welcome; it is quite legitimate for a new building to appear honestly as being both new and built. To fit well into an existing context does not mean to be invisible there.

Architecture often has an opportunity to relate to its surroundings by creating some of those surroundings, extending its design or some complementary design into the landscape. Platforms, steps, terraces, approach walks and drives, and gardens of all sorts can mediate between buildings and nature. And there is a realm of gazebos and pavilions, formal plantings, garden follies, man-made grottoes, hedges that are like walls, and cypresses that are like obelisks, in which the distinction between landscape and architecture is pleasantly blurred. A fountain design, for instance, while it lacks an interior space, is quite a worthy challenge for the skills of an architect, as Bernini amply showed, and may be as effective as any inhabited structure in galvanizing the space about it into a meaningful entity. And in some of the most beautiful villas of Italy (the word villa referring, significantly,

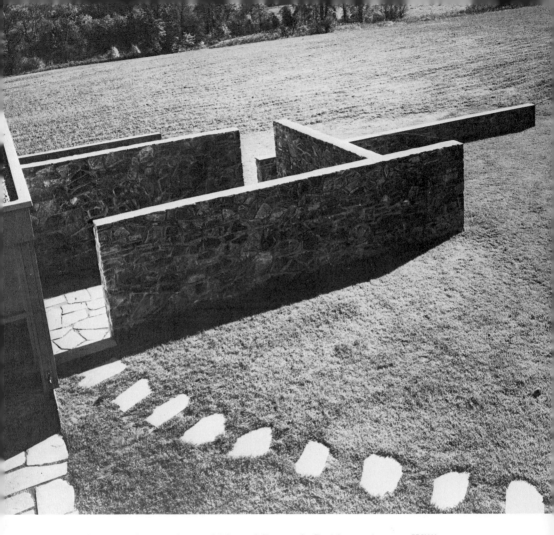

Outside the kitchen door of Marcel Breuer's Robinson house, Williamstown, Massachusetts: The fieldstone walls enclosing the service yard mediate between building and nature. (Robert Damora, courtesy Marcel Breuer Associates)

to the sum of country residence *and* its property), in the Villa Lante at Bagnaia, for example, or the Villa d'Este at Tivoli, or the Villa Torlonia at Frascati as it stands now, the landscaping is a much more powerful architectural element than any building.

(One of the most disappointing aspects of current practice is that artificial divisions of labor between architect and landscape architect and, similarly, between architect and sculptor and between architect and interior designer make it difficult for the same hand to design both a structure and its natural extensions. There are, fortunately, some exceptions.)

The temple of Surya, Modhera, India: the elaborate brick terraces stepping down toward an artificial lake assume an architectural importance rivaling that of the temple. (Photograph: Frederico Borromeo)

Another fundamental aspect of the thread-gathering process, unless the new building is in a wilderness or a desert, will relate that building to the older buildings around it, for they will already have made a substantial contribution to local character. A recall of local building tradition symbolizes continuity rather than rupture, the familiar rather than the strange, but it often has its practical merits as well, for such tradition will have grown up in response to climate and local building conditions. The side galleries of the houses of Charleston are positioned to shade the south or west windows and to catch the breezes from the sea; the adobe construction of New Mexico is insulation against radical changes of temperature; an English house, wanting light, may have larger window areas than a house in sunny Spain. There are also regional traditions based on past availability of building materials: from colonial times, a tradition of building with wood in Massachusetts, with stone in Pennsylvania, with brick in Georgia.

Awareness of these traditions is important, but the architect must beware of slavish imitation of them. Temperature can be controlled very well in New Mexico these days without thick walls, and brick is now as available as wood in Massachusetts. To build with regard to the restraints of two centuries ago and in defiance of current practicalities is not a valid basis for good architecture.

The cylindrical form of the Chiesa delle Maddalena in Venice is a compatible closure to the vista along the curving canal that approaches it. (Photograph: Stanley Abercrombie)

The Italian hill towns of Triora (left) and Andagna (right): Is the tower on the hill more effective than the tower somewhere else or the hill left bare? (Photograph: Norman F. Carver, Jr., AIA)

However it relates to its landscape and to its older neighbors, of course, a building has available to it those compositional rules that prevail at any scale. Not only in relating building elements to each other or to a whole, but also in relating new buildings to existing ones and to city plans in general, the principles of repetition, of proportion, and of complementary shapes have their contributions to make. As a drum-shaped enclosure serves to prepare us for a domed interior, so may such a drum serve as a focal point of axial vistas, or as a compatible incident in a series of curving passages.

Fitting a place is more than a matter of shape, however; it is a matter, as well, of choosing a suitable size, suitable finishes, and suitable attitudes. To be suitable is not necessarily to be identical with anything existing, for art can result as easily from contrast as from conformance. A major way in which architecture contributes to our environment is by making noteworthy contrast, providing that significant gesture that fixes and announces the importance of place. In this sort of dominant relationship of architecture over nature, as in others, the question to ask is the same as we might ask about two windows placed together, or two blocks of granite: Is the result of the combination better than either alone? Is the tower on the hill more effective than the tower somewhere else or the hill left bare?

It is a simple sort of question, and in the present fashion for building "contextually," it is one we may be tempted to overcomplicate. The tedious matching of new buildings to old—pattern to pattern, color to color, cornice line to cornice line (or, if a genuine cornice is too expensive, an imitation cornice line may be thought to suffice)—may at times be a reasonable way to design, but not always, and it can be treacherous, particularly in urban settings, for the context we have so laboriously matched may itself be subject to change.

Mies van der Rohe and Philip Johnson's Seagram Building, one of the supreme beauties of our time, is not the simple rectangular shaft it is sometimes imagined to be, but a rather complex shape that projects and extends the tower's east face so that it meets and exactly covers the lower mass of some respectable but undistinguished neoclassical buildings that fill the rest of the block. Now those buildings are coming down, to be replaced by a greater volume, and the original careful alignment is for nothing. In this case, the virtues of the Seagram Building are intact, but there is an implicit warning: We may be so intent on the matching process that we fail to consider the inherent esthetic qualities of our new building. Matching a neighbor does not produce art; the best work, like Seagram, has an independent excellence that remains apparent and understandable if the neighbor vanishes.

Nor is art produced by the matching of a building to its culture or to its climate, however satisfying such matching may be in other ways. Culture and climate are design determinants, certainly, and on them we must base some functional criteria, but not esthetic criteria. Architecture can even excel as powerful art despite a deplorably loose fit with these determinants.

Chandigarh, the new capital of the Punjab, was planned to be a model city. Its design was the product not only of the genius of Le Corbusier, but also of the considerable talents of other architects as well: Matthew Nowicki, working as consultant for the firm of Mayer &Whittlesey, and Maxwell Fry and Jane Drew of London (who did enlightened work for the housing sectors and who, indeed, brought Le Corbusier into the team). But, for some, Chandigarh today is a source of disillusionment and disappointment (see writings by Subhash Chakravarty in *Architecture Plus* and by Brent Brolin, for example). Yet Le Corbusier's three monumental structures, the Palace of Justice, the Secretariat, and the Assembly Hall, are marvelous architecture still, whether or not their concrete screens capture and reradiate the Punjab's intense heat, whether or not they resemble anything built in the area before. For these buildings achieve something more rare and finally more satisfying than increasing our comfort or reflecting tradition. They do what architecture alone is capable of: They create place. They give this new city a living image, powerful for both those who are there and those who have never been there. The great truncated cone atop the Assembly Hall, for example, is a magnificent object. When we see it repeated, (intentionally and respectfully, we imagine) in the work of Italian architect Aldo Rossi (in his designs for both the Muggio town hall and the Modena cemetery), we think at once of Chandigarh, and our spirits are lifted.

If respect for place is not the highest achievement of which architecture is capable, it still must be admitted that placement can affect a building's esthetic quality. We have said that an effective relationship of building to earth is fundamental to architecture, and that if that relationship is awkward there cannot be a perfectly satisfying result. An extension of this principle suggests that there may be esthetic implications in a building's relationship to a site's whole topography, both natural and built—sometimes to a whole city; sometimes, even, to a whole region, however different are the design processes in each case.

Only it must be remembered that architecture's role is not always to conform, but often to transform an existing site by its introduction of new elements. This environmental role is a key function of architecture, the one that travels farthest beyond the building shell, and one unavailable to the smaller arts. The esthetic success of architecture on a monumental scale, indeed, is often measured primarily by its successful function as an important newcomer in the environment. Here we mean, of course, not a practical sort of function, but the less

The Sea Ranch condominium on the California coast, designed by Charles Moore, Donlyn Lyndon, William Turnbull, and Robert Whitaker: "The interaction of the thing itself and its environment." (Photograph: Gerald Allen)

easily measured thread-gathering, place-marking, character-defining sort of function.

But what of architecture's more utilitarian and self-contained functions: Can they, as well, have esthetic implications? The answer is less clear and less positive than most "functionalists" would have us think.

Function

The aim of architecture is the creation of the perfect and therefore most beautiful efficiency.

Bruno Taut, Modern Architecture

But more convincing:

Architecture lasts because it is art and surpasses its use.

Gio Ponti, In Praise of Architecture

A three-question quiz:

1. Brunelleschi's Foundling Hospital in Florence, one of the first and most instructive buildings of the Italian Renaissance, was largely finished in 1427, but not completed and formally opened until January 25, 1445, and the function it was meant to serve, the care of orphans, did not begin until February 5, when the first foundling was left there. On which of these dates did the building become beautiful?

2. Three identical vaulted bays of the Market of Trajan stand side by side among the ruins of Rome. At the present moment one holds a shop selling postcards, slides, and books, a function not unlike the building's original function. The next has a quite different function, museum exhibition space, and the third, suspected of structural weakness, is not in use. Which bay is most esthetically pleasing?

Wood gazebo at the Citadel, Cairo: Not a particularly effective shelter against rain (in a climate with minimal rainfall, in any case) or even against the sun, the little structure's major functions are those of creating a visible event in the long citadel wall and of establishing a small but special environment. (Photograph: Stanley Abercrombie)

3. When the marble facing and bronze hardware were stripped from the Pantheon by Pope Urban VIII in the seventeenth century, the building's usefulness was not affected. Was its appearance changed?

Nonsensical questions, but not a bit more so than most of the theories that would tie esthetic value to the coattails of function. These theories are stated in two general ways: first, as in the quotation from the German Expressionist architect Bruno Taut, that a building that fulfills its function is therefore beautiful; second, that a building that fails to fulfill its function cannot be beautiful. And these two views imply a third: that, because form should be a by-product of function, it does not deserve the primary attention of the designer, and that architecture must therefore be merely an applied—not a fine—art. This view is reflected whenever we ask of a building, "Does it work?" and imagine that we are asking about esthetics; it is a question we never ask about painting, sculpture, or music except when they are being used as propaganda. And this view is also lurking beneath the attitude expressed by Walter Gropius that "the approach to any kind of design—a chair, a building, a whole town or a regional plan—should be essentially identical."

But we cannot design a building as we would a chair if we believe that architecture is a powerful art quite distinct from furniture. The idea of architecture as less than a fine art is too foreign to our experience to be acceptable. We know that it is not even true that architecture must always house a function. Mies van der Rohe's Barcelona pavilion, built for an exhibition in 1929 and then leveled, was never meant to house a function more useful or complex than a contemplative stroll among its carefully disposed planes of onyx, glass, and marble; yet the strength of its concept made it one of the most compelling prototypes in twentieth-century architecture.

Nor do the functions of architecture often continue unchanged. Town houses are converted into banks, breweries into concert halls, fire stations into art galleries, all without affecting the esthetic quality of whatever architecture remains. And some admired structures from antiquity are of unknown purpose.

Thomas Jefferson's rotunda is secure as the keystone of his masterful architectural composition at the University of Virginia, although it has been many years since the building was used for its originally intended function, that of a library and administration building. Thomas Schumacher, Associate Professor of Architecture at the university, has reported a campus story from the time of the building's restoration in 1976: A professor asked a groundskeeper what he thought

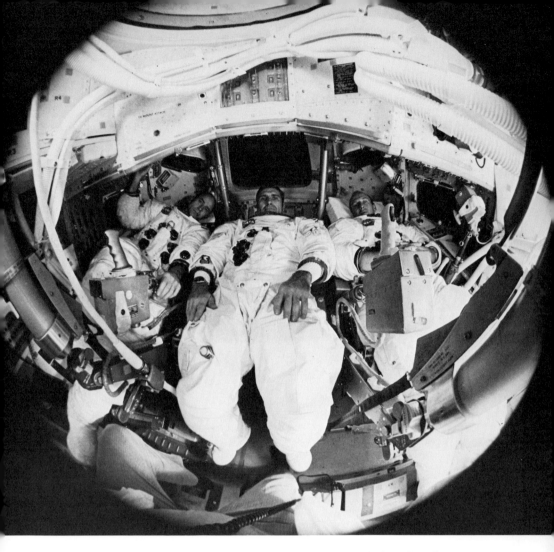

The spacecraft Apollo 12: A highly functional, carefully designed environment. It works, certainly, but no one would mistake it for architecture. (Photograph: National Aeronautics and Space Administration)

the building would be used for after its restoration. "I don't know," he said. "I guess they're going to use it for a rotunda."

Yet the persistence of functionalist views cannot be ignored. Edward Robert De Zurko's very useful book, *Origins of Functionalist Theory*, traces them chronologically from their classical origins to modern times and finds that all functionalist theories have been based on one of three analogies. These have much in common with three of the four "fallacies" deplored by English critic (and editor of Boswell's papers) Geoffrey Scott in *The Architecture of Humanism*, and, giving them the same names used by Scott, we can call them the mechanical analogy, the ethical analogy, and the biological analogy.

The mechanical analogy is implied in one of modern architecture's most frequently repeated catch-phrases, Le Corbusier's "A house is a machine for living in." Even before the industrial revolution inspired a rash of machine worship, Francis Hutcheson, in 1725, while teaching ethics at the University of Glasgow, proclaimed an esthetic pleasure in the workings of machines, demonstrating as they do both man's wisdom and his economy.

The ethical analogy has an even longer history. Socrates saw a relationship between beauty and usefulness; he also saw a relationship between usefulness and good. From Xenophon's *Memorabilia and Oeconomicus*, as translated by Marchant:

Socrates: You think, do you, that good is one thing and beautiful another? Don't you know that all things are both beautiful and good in relation to the same things . . . ?
Aristippus: Is a dung basket beautiful then?
Socrates: Of course, and a golden shield is ugly, if the one is well made for its special work and the other badly.

Plato saw similar correspondences. More recently, Alexander Pope, ridiculing the neo-Palladian houses of the early eighteenth century, reminded Lord Burlington that

'Tis use alone that justifies expense,
And splendour borrows all her rays from sense.

Pope's contemporary, the Earl of Shaftesbury, went so far as to state that the cultivation of artistic appreciation was a preparation for moral development.

The biological analogy is, perhaps, a little less direct. Geoffrey Scott used the term "biological fallacy" to refer to the misapplication to architecture of the natural phenomena of evolution, maturation, and decadence. An important strain of functionalist theory described by De Zurko can be said to depend on a different sort of analogy with biology. This strain was popular among the early modernists. For Frank Lloyd Wright, a work of architecture at its best was a single organism in which all parts are necessarily related in a functional way, and the great cliché of early modernism, "form follows function," had, of course, the sanction of the revered Louis Sullivan. It was a point of view strongly bolstered by the visual impact of the industrial revolution and its continuing development.

Yet, as Marcel Breuer pointed out in a 1948 lecture, "Sullivan did not eat his functionalism as hot as he cooked it." And Mies van der

Rohe said he wouldn't eat it at all: "We do the opposite," *Architectural Forum* quoted him as saying in 1952. "We reverse this, and make a practical and satisfying shape, and then fit the function into it. Today this is the only practical way to build, because the functions of most buildings are continually changing, but economically the buildings cannot change." Ruskin had even gone to an antifunctionalist extreme by maintaining that "the most beautiful things in the world are the most useless; peacocks and lilies for instance."

Still, to deny function any influence over esthetic value is to oversimplify the case. Architecture is not just a combination of function and art, but (as Roger Scruton, a lecturer in philosophy at Birkbeck College, London, recently pointed out in *The Aesthetics of Architecture*) a synthesis of the two. In what ways, then, do functional matters affect our esthetic judgment?

First of all, we like to see things at work (electric trains, circus acts, printing presses, the sculpture of Tinguely and Calder), and, second,

Two-headed term at Harding Circle, Sarasota, Florida: It displeases us as a lighting fixture because it does not appear to work efficiently, its base being disproportionately large for the tiny lamp it supports. (Photograph: Stanley Abercrombie)

we are pleased when we think things are working well. These inclinations combine so that we naturally like the look of things we think will work well. Horace Kallen, in *Art and Freedom,* points out that "the horse that has thin flanks is thought handsomer than one of a different shape, and is also more swift." But the thin-flanked horse is not necessarily proven to be more swift; we think him handsomer before we ever see him run. This anticipation of function is due to what Kant called our teleological way of thinking, our capacity to see the ends of things, to see, for another example, flight in the wings of birds. And this sort of thinking is at the heart of the esthetic pleasure architecture offers. It is admirable for a building to work well, but we do not admire it as art for working well; it is in looking *as if* it will work well that it gives us esthetic pleasure.

(Philip Johnson has remarked that visitors often make judgments about the comfort of the Mies van der Rohe funiture in his living room before they ever sit on it. If they find the Barcelona chair beautiful, they are inclined to find it comfortable as well, and vice versa.)

Leaving esthetics aside for a moment, it is worth pointing out that, even with function primarily in mind, the architect can design only what seems as if it would be best. A perfect functional fit requires an architect to be omniscient about both present and future. As design methodologist David Canter has written in the British *Architects' Journal,* "A building . . . is often designed to be a suitable setting for the activities carried out in it. An individual's idea of a suitable setting will relate to his notion of who does what in the setting. This might have nothing to do with what actually happens or with the best conditions for the performance of the real activities. . . . In short, the clients' satisfaction might depend more on the architects' psychological insight than on how adequate the 'brief' is."

Returning to the matter of a building's merely appearing to be functional, we have a right to expect of our architecture that it be well designed at least to the same degree and in the same way as are good toasters, good hair dryers, good typewriters, and other industrial objects. Principles of industrial design demand that tools and products be not only suitable for their purpose, but also that their suitability be apparent, that objects be not only operable, but also that the manner of their operation be clear (where we drop the coin, how we hold the handle, how we start the motor, where the cigarettes come out).

Being shown how to use a work of architecture is more complicated than being shown how to use most machines, and being persuaded that the architecture works well is also complicated, for although most machines have a single function, architecture must function in many

The Roman theater at Sagalassos: Form partially dictated by requirements for hearing and seeing. (Photograph: Fototeca Unione, Rome)

ways. These include, to begin with the most basic, the general function of sheltering, then the more specific accommodation of particular
activities, then the accommodation of circulation among those activities, then the mechanical function, the acoustic function (for some
building types), the structural function, the constructional function,
and, already mentioned, the function of a building in its environment.
At least a couple of these, the structural and constructional functions,
deserve a closer look.

The structural function is fundamental to architecture. We have
already considered the drama of a structure's effort to escape the pull
of gravity; when this effort is visually demonstrated, the result can
be thrilling. Art historian Erwin Panofsky, in an eloquent sentence
in *Scholasticism and Gothic Architecture*, tells how Gothic cathedrals
came to give us this sort of thrill: "Ultimately, the flying buttress
learned to talk, the rib learned to work, and both learned to proclaim

Above, the Brownlee house, Honolulu, designed by Wimberly, Whisenand, Allison, Tong and Goo; *right,* the Yamanashi Press and Radio Center, Kofu, by Kenzo Tange: Structural function visually demonstrated. (Photograph above: Wimberly, Whisenand, Allison, Tong and Goo; right photograph: Masao Arai, courtesy The Japan Architect Co., Ltd.)

what they were doing in a language more circumstantial, explicit and ornate than was necessary for mere efficiency."

One structural attitude that is often worthy of celebration is a building's basic act of supporting itself and its contents. When a building is big, this is never a simple or casual matter. But less typical attitudes,

like unusual athletic feats or dance steps, are more appropriately dramatized. The cantilever is one of these, actually a sensible and efficient way of loading a beam, but one that leaves an architectural
burden projecting beyond its vertical support. When that support is
perched on the edge of a cliff, as in the case of a house at Cuenca,
Spain (now, incidentally, converted into a museum), the effect can
be spectacular.

Another unusual structural gesture, the exceptionally tall building,

A house at Cuenca, Spain: The drama of a cantilevered structure exaggerated
by the cliff below. (Photograph: Norman F. Carver, Jr., AIA)

Abner Pratt's 1860 "Honolulu House" in Marshall, Michigan: The jigsawed brackets refer to a necessary connection between porch roof and supporting columns, but they are not necessarily themselves the connection. (Photograph: Balthazar Korab)

can be thought of as a vertical cantilever, braced in this case not against the earth's gravity but against high winds and other earth-related forces, like a paddle held steady in a swift river. These buildings of unexpected horizontal projection or unexpected vertical extension are the simplest of the architect's vocabulary of striking structural gestures. Others include great arches, vaults, and domes and, for diagonal forces, complex trusses, braces, and buttresses. There are far too many to mention, and, for each, both appropriate and inappropriate forms for demonstrating its use.

Structurally, what counts is that the building stands. Esthetically, what counts is only the demonstration. Even ancient Greek architecture, the epitome of beautifully expressed structure, is not by any means structurally exact or spare. Joseph Gwilt, a nineteenth-century observer, detected in Greek temples the principle "that no support should be burthened with a greater quantity of matter than itself contains," but this is not a particularly rigorous structural principle. Rhys Carpenter noted that even though there are "no structural irrelevancies" in the temples, "neither is there much structural inventiveness or ambition." Greek building never even attempted to approach the structural limits of its material.

In later times, other architectural delights are even more clearly nonstructural—for example, the elaborate jigsawed brackets of the American "Victorian" house. They may refer to a necessary connection between porch roof and supporting columns, but they are not themselves the connection. Take them away, and the house becomes less interesting, less expressive, less artful; yet the roof does not fall.

In our own time, looking up at Skidmore,Owings & Merrill's John Hancock tower in Chicago, we see the prominent cross-bracing and receive an impression of building strength exerted against natural forces. We do not know if every bracing member we see is actually working as it appears to be; unless we set to work with all the information and all the ability of the Hancock's structural engineer (the late Fazlur Khan), we cannot know. Never mind, the appearance suffices. What would be esthetically disruptive is a member that appeared weak, no matter what its actual strength.

Some industrial and military structures perform extraordinary structural feats, and our common sense tells us that they must have been engineered to be sound, but they have not been designed to appear sound. The British "sea forts" built during World War II, for example, balance habitable units atop spindly legs rising from the sea; there surely must be a safe connection between the units and the legs, yet the connection is awkward and ungainly. We may not fear a structural

Skidmore, Owings & Merrill's John Hancock Center, Chicago: We cannot know if each visible brace is working as it appears to be, but the appearance is nevertheless satisfying. (Photograph: Bill Engdahl, Hedrich-Blessing)

World War II "sea forts": Presumably, the habitable units are attached securely to the long legs below, but the connection is visually unsatisfactory. (Photograph: Imperial War Museum, London)

failure, but the top and bottom of this composition are incompatible, and the object as a whole has no chance at art.

The obverse of this complaint is that apparent structural instability can be made, by the artist, into an asset. The "Cloud Props" proposed by El Lissitzky and Mart Stam in 1924 revel in the daring cantilever of useful floors over the slender base. If these structures had been built, we might well have worried about their safety, but we most likely would have cheered their artful bravado.

Constructional functionalism is similar to structural functionalism, but deals with elements that are assembled to form buildings rather than with the elements that bind them together. In older building methods, these were often the same elements; today they seldom are. Here again, it is the exceptional element that provides the best opportunity for the exercise of design. Henry-Russell Hitchcock and Philip Johnson, discussing Eero Saarinen's General Motors Technical Center in "The Buildings We See," 1952, wrote, "As has always been the case with industrial buildings, the more specialized functions of certain units provide the most interesting elements for the architect to organize visually. Thus the engine test-cell building, with its rows of round paired stacks on either side, has the most individual character and also the highest quality architecturally." It is a phenomenon not limited to industrial buildings, nor is it true only in the context of a spare architectural style starved for complexity. As Le Corbusier put it in "If I Had to Teach You Architecture," a 1938 article, " . . . the more modest the problem, the more imagination you need."

But modest constructional problems can be dramatized as well. No

A drawing (superimposed on a photograph) of El Lissitzky and Mart Stam's "Cloud Props" project for Moscow: Daring and visually compelling, whether or not the towers, if built, would have been safe.

Roman aqueduct, Segovia: The fitting together of constituent parts is at the heart of the art of architecture. (Photograph: Herbert Beckhard)

building is monolithic, no matter what its form, and the fitting together of its constituent parts consumes much of the architect's attention. Fitting can be expedient or it can be deeply felt. At its best, architecture conveys an acute sensitivity to the nature of different sorts of joints and connections and to the nature of the materials being joined. In *Stones of Rimini,* art critic Adrian Stokes considers limestone and imagines "fantasies of life in watery depths." And consider Ruskin's famous reaction to the materials of the porches surrounding St. Mark's in Venice:

Round the walls of the porches there are set pillars of variegated stones, jasper and porphyry, and deep-green serpentine spotted with flakes of snow, and marbles, that half refuse and half yield to the sunshine, Cleopatra-like, "their bluest veins to kiss"—the shadow, as it steals back from them, revealing line after line of azure undulation, as a receding tide leaves the waved sand . . . and above them, in the broad archivolts, a continuous chain of language and of life . . . and above these, another range of glittering pinnacles, mixed with white arches edged with scarlet flowers,—a confusion of delight . . . until at last, as if in ecstasy, the crests of the arches break into a marble foam, and toss themselves far into the blue sky in flashes and wreaths of sculptured spray, as if the breakers on the Lido shore had been frost-bound before they fell, and the sea-nymphs had inlaid them with coral and amethyst.

Few architects express their thoughts with the flair of Stokes or Ruskin, of course, but most architects exercise comparable imagination about the materials of construction, and it is imagination founded on knowledge of the materials' origin, of their strength, of their reaction to rain, dust, abrasion, painting, and carving, and of their feel to the human hand. This last—the touch of architecture—is a functional aspect not to be neglected.

Whatever value architecture may have as an exemplary treatment of materials, as a marker in the landscape, as a structure, or as enclosure, and whatever the esthetic implications of those functions, we must remember that, independent of any of them, it is also capable of eliciting esthetic response directly from our minds by its mere being. This role is not antifunctional; it is simply another function, an important one. And none of these values and functions is knowable by us except through the medium of our mental activity. "The world is my idea," Schopenhauer claimed, and it exists "only as a representation, in other words, only in reference to another thing, namely that which represents . . . "—namely ourselves. Architecture, and all the rest of the world, is, for each of us, our own construction.

Perception

All beauty is relative to the sense of some mind perceiving it.

Francis Hutcheson, *System of Moral Philosophy*

While many aspects of the art of architecture are highly subjective, the act of perceiving a building is part of our own biology, thus part of science. We might therefore assume its operation to be a steady fact, variable in our understanding of it, but in itself invariable. This is not exactly the case. While our eye structures and brain capacities persist unchanged, the use we make of ourselves is subject to great change, and such change colors the mechanics of our perception.

Very long ago, there was the fundamental change from primitive man, primarily interested in the space about him, to literate man, also interested in time and therefore able to see space in a new way; then the change from man's thinking himself to be the static center of the universe to his seeing himself, in the words of Pierre Teilhard de Chardin, "as the axis and leading shoot of evolution, which is something much finer"; then, even more recently, a refocusing of attention away from exterior facts and into his own feelings about those facts. In his introduction to E. M. Cioran's *The Fall Into Time,* Charles Newman refers to "the progressive disrealization of the world which began in the Renaissance." Disrealization: the intercession, between nature and art, of man's own rationality. Thus self-concerned, as a result of this most recent change, we enjoy the consideration of those personal responses that are conscious and voluntary, but we are sometimes

Hadrian's Villa, Tivoli: The entertaining game of supplying missing parts. (Photograph: Stanley Abercrombie)

disconcerted by those workings of our body that, however personal, are independent of our will. Visual perception, or some large part of it, is one of these, no matter what use we make of its results.

It is an oversimplification, but perhaps a useful one, to consider that we establish for ourselves the character of a building or of any other object by compiling information gathered in two ways. The first way is a chain of physical activities that are responses to the light refracted to us from the built form: The receptors (called rods and cones) in our eyes react to the light by releasing ions, thus producing a bioelectric signal that moves through the optic nerve to two areas of our brain (called the superior colliculus and the striate cortex). These areas analyze the sighted object's placement, form, and motion, and in turn pass that information along to other parts of the brain by means of changes in the nerve cells' electrical activity.

Automatic as it may be, this is not a simple way of gathering information. It begins not in a single act, such as the opening of the shutter of a camera, but in a series of related acts of focusing and refocusing, all requiring the exercise and control of tiny eye muscles. Thus some objects are seen with relative difficulty, while others are literally "easy on the eyes," being the primary forms that Le Corbusier said "are beautiful forms because they can be clearly appreciated." Any object with dimension—that is, anything more than a dot—is seen not at once but at the end of a kinesthetic process. This is true of two-dimensional art, our eyes traveling along a line or about a painting; it is true to a greater extent of architecture, which, almost always, will be fully perceived only after we have carried our perceiving eyes around and through it.

The second way of gathering information may have already taken place before the first is finished, for, unless we have never looked at any other building, some of the information will be stored, awaiting use, in other brain cells. This is information of a general type, with which we can compare one building with another: information about size, shape, placement, and purpose, as well as less essential information such as the building's cost, the name of its builder, its architect, its rental agent, its neighborhood, and the fact that our grandmother once lived in a building very much like it.

The first sort of perception, an automatic reaction to the visible building, is the basis of our esthetic response; the second sort, more circumstantial, modifies and complicates that response. Even if it were possible, it would be foolish to ask our brains to censor out the second sort of information, for some supplementation of the raw facts is useful, even when it is accomplished not only with stored-up circumstantial facts but also with our emotions, prejudices, and dispositions at the moment of perception. As neurophysiologist Dr. Heinz Von Foerster pointed out in his keynote address to the 1975 convention of the American Institute of Architects, "The sensors . . . do not report to you the physical act which brought them to operate. They only report the quantity, not the quality. . . . The central nervous system does not receive any clues as to what caused the discharge of the sensory nerves." We need the second sort of information, therefore, to explain the first. As Kant said in *The Critique of Pure Reason*: "The senses cannot think. The understanding cannot see. By their union only can knowledge be produced."

Even so, for the best appreciation of architecture, we should beware of allowing the visual evidence of built form to become obscured by nonvisual data. What our eyes tell us about a building is never the whole truth, but it is a crucial part of the truth. Even as acute an observer as Thomas Jefferson could be blinded to the Virginia vernacular of his youth by the fact that he wished it to be replaced by a different, more "correct" style. Of the private houses of Williamsburg, now pilgrimage sites for thousands, he wrote that "It is impossible to devise things more ugly, uncomfortable, and—happily—more perishable." William and Mary College and the adjacent hospital for lunatics were, in his mind, "rude, misshapen piles, which, but that they have roofs, would be taken for brick-kilns," and of colonial American architecture in general he said that "The first principles of the art are unknown, and there exists scarcely a model among us sufficiently chaste to give an idea of them." Williamsburg has changed since Jefferson's time, of course. The Duke of Gloucester Street is now paved, and there are no longer any pigs wandering about. But we have changed as well: In our own time, we may easily be blinded to the actual form of the same buildings for opposite reasons and with opposite effects, because we are so enthusiastic about the correctness of their style and because they have, for us, such charm.

One positive way in which this mental supplementation of visual facts can operate is in our searching for fundamental simplicities—for underlying symmetry, for example—when the forms we see exhibit such simplicities imperfectly. Looking through the gate at Lord Burlington's Chiswick House, what we see is the main body of the house and, to its right but not to its left, an adjoining pavilion. The whole view is therefore not quite in balance, yet it is so close to being so that our impression is definitely one of symmetry. In other cases, such as Alberti's Palazzo Ruccellai in Florence, seeing a fragment, we imagine a whole. Our perceptual supplementation in these ways helps art along: We look for compositional logic.

At the same time, the architect may be helping us find such logic, paradoxically, by deviating from logical form. Responding to the fact that man's eye level is far below the top of a temple, the architect may tilt the entablature of the temple slightly foward, not enough so that we sense the tilt, but enough so that we see clearly the full size of the building. And one explanation (but not the only one) of all the almost imperceptible "refinements" of a Greek temple is that they are designed to correct the optical illusions that could result from more regular spacings, more uniformly tapered columns, and more level surfaces. Another explanation of the same subtle distortions is that

Chiswick House, London: A pavilion at the right side of the house is not balanced by another at the left, yet our first impression is one of perfect symmetry. (Photograph: Stanley Abercrombie)

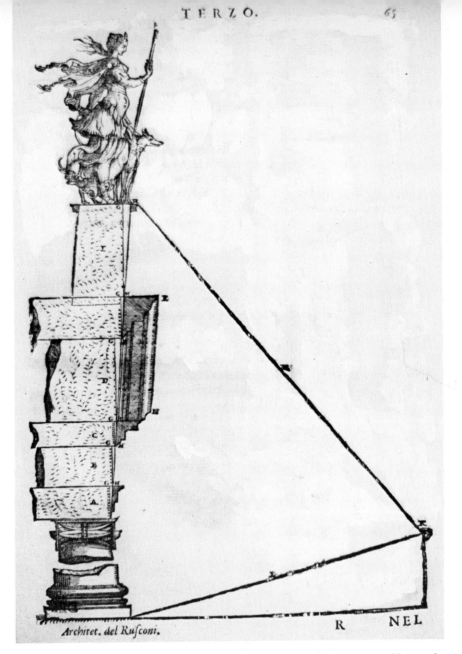

Architet. del Rusconi.

R NEL

From Rusconi's *dell'Architettura*, a drawing suggesting that an entablature be tilted forward an imperceptible degree so that its size might be more comprehensible from eye level. (Courtesy American Academy in Rome)

they are meant to suggest a humanlike counterthrust to the weight of the structure—the upward push of the stylobate, for example, or the bulging metaphorical muscle of the column's entasis. Whether either or both of these explanations is close to the intentions of the

Frank Lloyd Wright's Guggenheim Museum: A stage for the inspection of our fellow creatures from unusual vantage points. (Robert E. Mates, courtesy The Solomon R. Guggenheim Museum)

Greek architects, the resultant architecture is enriched by the irregularities that effectively manipulate our perception.

It is also true that, much as we may seek completed and logical forms, there is a value in the irregularities that prevent our finding such forms too easily. Desmond Morris, in *The Human Zoo*, has described man's acute need, in order to ensure his full development, for finding a variety of stimuli—and not just easy answers—in his environment. Similarly, studies at the University of Montreal some years ago indicated that either overstimulation or understimulation can be damaging to the central nervous system.

But architecture is not only an object to be perceived; it also serves as a stage for our perception of other objects. Depending on the building type, these objects can be smaller artworks, dances, operas, or liturgies. Independent of building type, however, architecture is always a stage for our perception of other people. We like to see—or, at least, to imagine—people in built spaces, and those buildings have an extra interest for us that allow us to see people in unusual views.

Great spaces, interior or exterior, let us view people at great distance; small ones force us into intimacy. Vertical shafts allow us to look down on people from above; ramps and stairs display people moving diagonally. Whatever its faults or virtues in showing us paintings, Wright's Guggenheim Museum affords us a supreme architectural experience because of the fascinating variety of ways in which it shows us other people (and, through them, of course, ourselves) from above, below, and across the continuous spiral.

Such display of the human body is one of architecture's enduring sources of delight, for our curiosity about our own bodies is apparently insatiable. Architecture is also measured by the body: it is through the use of ourselves as reference that we perceive architecture's size and character. Architects Charles Moore and Gerald Allen, in their book *Dimensions*, have clarified the troublesomely vague term *scale*, so often used by architects in describing the size of buildings; a chapter by Allen explains that scale simply means "*relative* size." It is therefore, perhaps, an almost always unnecessary word, for our perception of size is always relative to something else—to neighboring buildings or building elements, at times, but always and primarily to the human body. If ever we make friends with nonhuman creatures from another part of the universe, or if ever we come upon the architecture they have left behind, one of the problems to be overcome will be their size relative to our own and, because our esthetic judgment is founded on our own size, their inevitable ugliness.

Architecture, then, is a perceptible object, a stage for other tangible objects, and a parade ground for ourselves. It is also a means through which we learn intangible information. Here we leave the largely mechanical perception of visual phenomena and encounter the more complex perception of meaning.

The Meaning of Architecture

Architecture as a fine art has nothing to do with arts of
expression. . . . The business of buildings is not to tell tales
about the world . . . or of humanity, or of theology.

> Russell Sturgis, "Address," in *American Architect and Building News*, 1890

But:

Art always was and must remain a mode of symbolic
discourse, and where there is no symbol and therefore no
discourse, there is no art.

> Herbert Read, "The Disintegration of Form in Modern Art,"
> in *The Origins of Form in Art*

Architecture is both of the world and about the world. It never
simply exists; it also communicates; it has content; it conveys messages. The most obvious of these messages are the ones we might
call denotative. They are explicit and specific. Perhaps the most familiar building of our time that is wholly devoted to the delivery of
this sort of message is a little stand on the eastern end of Long Island,
first shown by Peter Blake in *God's Own Junkyard* and then further
popularized by Robert Venturi, Denise Scott Brown, and Steven Ize-

Engaged papyrus columns, Sakkara: These plant form imitations in stone from
the third millenium B.C. are simple but extraordinarily realistic, their shafts
being, like papyrus stems, triangular in section, swelling just above the ground
and tapering gently toward the fanning capitals that resemble plant heads.
(Photograph: Stanley Abercrombie)

nour in their book *Learning from Las Vegas*; it is a stand that sells ducks and duck eggs and is itself shaped like a duck.

Denotative meaning is not always so understandable. A chain of gas stations in the American south was once designed to resemble icebergs; there is no knowing why. Nor is denotative meaning always intentional. The lowest form of architectural criticism (but an entertaining one, sometimes) is accusing a building of looking like something else. One might say, for example, that Edward Durrell Stone's museum building at Columbus Circle, New York, with its borders of round holes, looks a bit like a page torn from a spiral binder, and when the *Journal of the Royal Institute of British Architects* featured Le Corbusier's La Tourette monastery, then under construction, on its front cover, an unappreciative reader responded that "it looks rather like a Coal Sorting Depot designed by a structural engineer for the Coal Board." But the game of "looks like" must not be taken seriously.

The medieval cathedral was a deeply serious compilation of similarly explicit messages. Substituting as a bible for a largely illiterate congregation, it was covered with artworks that told bible stories. However admirable some of these works may have been as sculpture or mosaic

Capitals in the cloister of the Duomo, Monreale, Sicily: Architecture as a framework for the presentation of bible stories. (Photograph: Fototeca Unione, Rome)

or stained glass, what we value most in medieval architecture is a quality wholly independent of the little stories it framed.

The cathedral as a whole, of course, also had an obvious denotative meaning of its own; a "sermon in stone," it was often big enough, in relationship to the town around it, to preach its sermon over the rooftops and out into the countryside. A sermon, whether verbal or masonry, is not art, but propaganda; the two can coexist but never touch. "We hate poetry that has a palpable design upon us," Keats said.

Similarly, we can appreciate Italian architect Giuseppe Terragni's Casa del Fascio in Como as a three-dimensional composition in which planar facades are manipulated to indicate the spaces beyond them, and such appreciation is distinct from our lack of sympathy for the fascist party it housed. Success as a recognizable building type—church or party headquarters—is not success as art, and success in establishing a point of view of "the world, or of humanity, or of theology" is even more foreign. We might even say that we cannot clearly see a building as a possible work of art until we close our eyes to its denotative meanings. Admiring the bright marquees and dazzling neon signs of Broadway, G. K. Chesterton is said to have exclaimed, "Oh, what a paradise this might be if only someone were unable to read!"

What we value about a medieval cathedral, however, is not independent of a more subtle, connotative sort of meaning. This is primarily a message about its own remarkable construction and the way it holds itself up. The cathedral is architecture with work to do—throwing walls of stone far up to enclose unreasonably tall voids, while bracing those walls only from the outside and while also puncturing them for light—and that work is naturally its own primary subject matter.

In other buildings, primary connotative meanings can concern other sorts of structure, building quality in general, rightness of proportion, attention to detail, or the appropriate use of material. To some extent, building materials and techniques are not only means to practical ends, but also ends in themselves. The architect's task, as Louis Sullivan wrote, is "to vitalize building materials, to animate them collectively with a thought, a state of feeling, to charge them with a subjective significance. . . ." And Le Corbusier, similarly, said that "The business of Architecture is to establish emotional relationships by means of raw materials." This ideal is not easily achieved (a tall door is not automatically stately; a yellow room is not always cheerful) for emotional relationships are personal and sometimes elusive.

The connotative meanings of buildings can be manipulated by the architect to suggest something about the building's owners or its ten-

IBM headquarters, Le Gaude, France; Marcel Breuer, architect; Robert Gatje, associate: Building structure animated by an implicit comparison with the human body at work. (Robert Mottar, courtesy Marcel Breuer Associates)

James Thurber's drawing of "Home": "The business of Architecture is to establish emotional relationships. . . ." (Copyright © 1943 James Thurber. Copyright © 1971 Helen W. Thurber and Rosemary T. Sauers. From *The Seal in the Bedroom,* Harper & Row.)

ants or its use. These meanings can imply a character that is nature loving or one that is urbane, gregarious or withdrawn, progressive or conservative. Skidmore, Owings & Merrill's Lever House is scrubbed and shiny without any literal, denotative reference to soap. Frank Lloyd Wright's Johnson Wax headquarters has a smooth, polished look. The New Jersey buildings of Johnson & Johnson by I. M. Pei and others have an air of being both antiseptic and trustworthy. Eero Saarinen's Dulles airport near Washington suggests the essence of flight (although the same architect's earlier TWA terminal in New York attempts the same effect in a more literal, clumsy way and is clearly a "duck").

The Venturi group began *Learning from Las Vegas* with this statement: "The morality of commercial advertising, gambling interests, and the competitive instinct is not at issue here." Fair enough. Even

The D. H. Day farm, Glen Haven, Michigan: Commonplace forms made unusually expressive, almost baronial. Compared with plainer barns, this one is highly suggestive of its builder's character. (Photograph: Balthazar Korab)

though the presence of such elements may be unattractive, their morality is another matter, more complicated, more personal, and irrelevant to building quality. "Art is the right way of doing right things," W. R. Lethaby thought, but it is probably closer to the truth to say that art is simply the right way of doing things. "There is no such thing as a moral or an immoral book," Oscar Wilde said in his preface to *Picture of Dorian Gray.* "Books are well written, or badly written . . . . The moral life of man forms part of the subject-matter of the artist, but the morality of art consists in the perfect use of an imperfect medium." Even those who feel certain that church attendance is more moral than gambling can imagine an ugly church and an artful casino.

Although morality or immorality is not taught by architecture, architecture does nevertheless transmit much of its creators' attitudes. Gambling halls as well as churches speak to us in various tones of voice that have nothing to do with the buildings' intended functioning, but only with the manner of that functioning. One thing we can learn from the casinos of Las Vegas or Atlantic City is man's capacity for rapaciousness; his capacity for grace and style we can learn from those of Baden-Baden or Cannes.

Such built personalities originate in a combination of sources, primarily in the values of clients, builders, and general society. The personalities inform us about those sources, and such sociological information is part of the meaning of any work of architecture.

It is possible to overinterpret architecture, of course, to infer a civilization from trivia. An extreme example is this paragraph from *The American Architect and Building News* of 1878:

The national character of a people is expressed in its dress and its ornaments in the same manner that handwriting carries with it the character of the writer. For example, take the English, the French, and the German. In England the leaders of fashion, etc., are from twenty to thirty years old; in France, old and young alike interest themselves; in Germany, the old professor gives the tone in art matters. Now take a coat of each and note the characteristics of the people in the cut of it: the English, square and angular; the French, graceful and soft in its lines; and the German has some of the former, and adds some scholasticism inclining to the pedantic. Take, again, the treatment of a simple trefoil by the different peoples; and we find the first is all vigor, nearly everything in straight lines; the second is all grace and elegance; the last, with some vigor (sharp corners), and some grace in the motion, has the scholasticism in the central divisions, which must all have the convex and concave sweep.

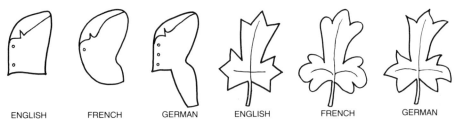

ENGLISH   FRENCH   GERMAN   ENGLISH   FRENCH   GERMAN

After *The American Architect and Building News* of 1878: National characters as revealed in the designs of waistcoats and of trefoils.

Obviously, not only whole buildings but parts of buildings (such as trefoils) can convey meaning. Ammanati's heavy rustication on the Pitti Palace does something more than add visual interest to a broad building form that, if left bare, would be ponderous; its rich texture of light and shadow also tells us something about the intensity of the Florentine sun. This pattern is ornament speaking a language of its own: It is climate made visible.

Ammanati's heavy rustication on the Pitti Palace, Florence: Its rich texture of light and shadow tells us something about the intensity of the Florentine sun. (Photograph: Stanley Abercrombie)

(Ruskin even attributed some measure of the power of architecture to the quantity, measured either in area or in intensity, of its shadow, an aspect of building design he labeled "Rembrandtism" and one obviously related not only to a building's size but also, in the case of dark openings, to the vigor of its modeling.)

Other ornamental patterns convey other kinds of information. As buildings age, their surfaces begin to tell us of the forces of nature that have been acting upon them. Staining and weathering, channeled by the modeling of the facade, bear evidence of wind, soot, rain, and of the relative hardness of the building materials employed.

Texture can also provide a building with a quality we recognize as human, for we ourselves live intimately with our own textures. The character of a fingerprint pleases us more than the character of a rubber glove. Alvar Aalto was exceptionally adept at the humanizing of his buildings by texture, and he was conscious also that all building materials have characteristic temperature ranges, some more appealing than others. He gave us steel columns, for example, that are cased in leather just for that part of their height that might be brushed against by building users.

There is no justification, obviously, for suggesting that the rough is always preferable to the smooth. Some of our finest architecture derives much of its brilliance from its sleek, machined surfacing. Nor would one ever suggest that texture alone can raise a building into art. It can, however, raise a building from ordinariness into particularity. Roger Fry's *Last Lectures* described a similar role performed by tactile elements in painting, and he might well have been writing of the Pitti Palace: "If the general plan is more or less conformable to a geometric idea the mind might be tempted to apprehend it merely as a case of a generalization (as it apprehends a diagram in Euclid); but the perpetual slight variations of surface keep the mind and attention fixed in the world of sensation." This much, at least, seems true: that texture, like larger ornamental effects (for texture is only ornament at a very fine grain) is both a potential detriment and a potential asset to architecture.

Some of the message a building conveys has its roots in conditions over which the architect has little power. Although, in the early stages of a project, an enlightened and energetic architect can work to educate the client, to fight restrictive codes and customs, or to persuade com-

Precast concrete panel detail, James Stirling's St. Andrews University dormitory: Texture provides a building with a quality we recognize as human. The character of a fingerprint pleases us more than the character of a rubber glove. (Photograph: James Stirling)

Palladio's Villa Capra, near Vicenza: The villa oversees the surrounding landscape on all sides, an attitude made more explicit by the statuary. (Photograph:
Stanley Abercrombie)

munities to accept previously unpopular improvements, he or she will in the end be required to design a given program of spatial requirements at a given location within given laws for a given budget. Even within these limits, however, the architect can exercise some choice; writing of "Modern Architectural Theory and the Liturgy" in Peter Hammond's *Towards a Church Architecture*, Nigel Melhuish has pointed out that "the notion that we could predict the future if we knew the position of every particle in the universe has long been abandoned by science, but a similar idea persists in architecture: that if you knew all the relevant facts, you could determine the shape of your building. The trouble is that 'relevance' is largely governed by the designer's statement of the problem: it depends on his point of view." The exercise of this point of view is the saving factor that makes architecture more than a science, and the particular choices an architect makes give a building another type of connotative meaning: information about the architect and about his or her attitude toward that building's users.

The most obvious way in which such an attitude is manifested is simply the degree of care that the architect bothers to take. Commissions can be fulfilled in an expedient way or in a thoughtful way. Considering only those cases in which architects are perfect models of care, there still is a range of messages that can be communicated, messages that speak as clearly of an architect's character as would a month spent with him in the intimacy of a prison cell, and which we can all read with no knowledge whatsoever of the science of signs. Does an architect respect his clients, tolerate them, or despise them? Does he wish to elevate spirits and delight senses, or is his primary concern the efficient functioning of the entire society, suppressing personal excitations? Does he design simplistic functional objects without wit or intelligence—in other words, does he underestimate us? Does he condescend? Does he brag? Has he provided just the degree of intellectual stimulation we are capable of appreciating, or is his building, pretending to deliver more than it can, pompous? Daring too little, is it a bore?

This biographical revelation is not a primary message of the building, and it is not a primary contributor to esthetic value, but it might be said that the art of architecture is given an opportunity to flourish only when architects reveal themselves to be considerate and thoughtful. This is secondary information, then, about the architect rather than directly about his or her building, but it is information not without some relevance. "*Finnegans Wake* is about *Finnegans Wake*," the late Joyce scholar William York Tyndall wrote; nevertheless, we do not

The domed salon of Victor Horta's 1895 Van Eetvelde house, Brussels: Plant forms used structurally and thus made to embody a plant/building analogy. (Photograph: Bildarchiv Foto Marburg)

object that the novel also tells us something about James Joyce and something about his "ideal reader."

There are other secondary messages conveyed by architecture. Even when they are not meant to tell a specific, denotative story, representational elements have been incorporated into architecture since its beginning: animal forms, plant forms, the forms of man himself. Sometimes these are laden with a special significance, as the plant forms in Art Nouveau architecture were at times made to perform structurally and thus embody a plant/building analogy. Sometimes these forms, slight as they are, have a little coded reference for the initiated: in Renaissance Italy, a beehive form representing the patronage of the Barberini family, a fleur-de-lis the Farnese, a cluster of five spheres the Medici.

Sometimes natural forms persist in sophisticated building because they were the source for similar building in more primitive methods: stone capitals and abaci that recall the bundles of reeds and blocks

A molded brick from Louis Sullivan's 1884 Rubin Rubel house, Chicago: Architecture interpreting nature in an early example of Art Nouveau's whiplash curve. (Photograph: Stanley Abercrombie)

Columns from the hypostyle hall of Roger C. Ferri's Pedestrian City proposal: A contemporary application of plant forms to architecture. (Photograph: Roger C. Ferri)

of wood that were their precedents. This is architecture speaking to us not about its future but about its past, not about its potential use but about its origin. "There is," according to Henry James, not only the telling of "the story of one's hero," but also, "the story of one's story," and architecture, too, has its story to tell.

To continue the metaphor of language, these embellishments may have nothing specific to tell us, but may instead represent a manner of speaking. Architecture may be said to shout at times, at other times

Opposite, top: The Belvedere, St. Peter's, Rome: Architecture enlivened with a combination of plant, animal, and human forms. (Photograph: Fototeca Unione, Rome)

Opposite, bottom: Capital, Sant'Antimo, Montalcino, Italy: Creatures can exist in architecture that were never seen in life. (Photograph: George Cserna)

to engage us in polite discourse, and often to ramble incoherently. And such patterns of speech change with the times and with situations; we do not use today the language of Spenser or Shakespeare, and we do not address the garage mechanic in rhyming couplets. Although ways of speaking change, however, the ideas that we exchange with one another are as constant as the human condition is. Manners of communication must not be confused with the matters being communicated, and, just as pretty talk without content is of little worth, so is the ornamentation of clumsy building forms.

As we would expect, built references are most affecting for us when

Nirvana House, Fujisawa, Kanagawa prefecture, Japan, by architect Takefumi Aida: It is natural for us to identify faces and facial expressions wherever possible. (Taisuke Ogawa, courtesy The Japan Architect Co., Ltd.)

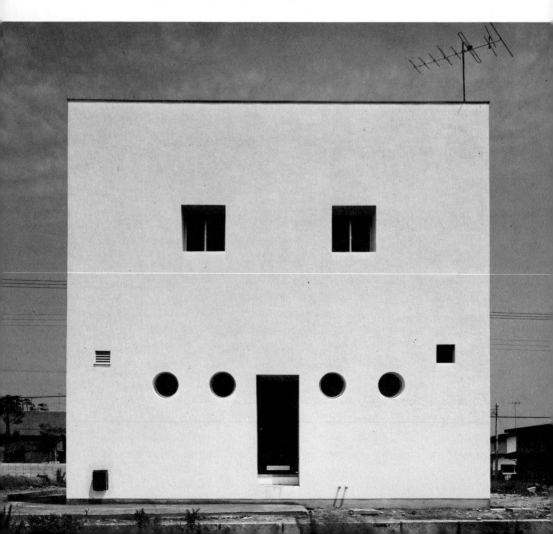

The stupa of Swayambunath, Nepal: The eyes painted on all four sides of the
tower keep watch imperiously over the Katmandu Valley. (Photograph: T. S.
Satyan, Camera Press, London)

they represent our own little province of nature, the human form, particularly the face. Even when such representations are unintended, we see parallels of our own features in buildings: The roof may be seen as a sheltering thatch of hair, windows are often seen as watching eyes, doorways are like mouths. These are associations so obvious that we are not likely to insult ourselves by bringing them into our consciousness often, but they are clearly in our minds, somewhere below the surface, and the architect does best not to deny them. Given our tendency to find faces wherever possible—in clouds and in puddles, as well as in facades—it is natural that we would also identify facial expressions and the emotions they represent: A building may appear to us to be friendly or fierce, contemplative or surprised. These associations are damaging only when, unsuspected by the architect, they establish a building character at odds with the intentions.

Building elements may also be personified without a direct resemblance. In one sense, a column may be thought to represent man, a sheltering arch woman. In another, temples to the strong gods such as Mars and Hercules were traditionally designed in the robust Doric order, while the more delicate Corinthian was considered proper for divinities such as Venus and Flora. In still another sense, Vasari compared a palazzo's facade to a man's face, its courtyard to his trunk, and its staircases to his arms and legs. Such connotative meanings, such associations and personifications are not the main meat of architecture, but they can add much to its flavor, and the skillful architect has always made use of them.

One example is the house designed by Robert Venturi in 1962 (and built in 1964) for his mother. It is a little building bristling with idiosyncrasies, but it nevertheless is meant to remind the observer of a stereotype house. And it is indeed—with its pitched roof, central chimney, and central door—close to the sort of house a child would draw. "I like to think . . ." Venturi has said, "that it achieves [an] essence, that of the genre that is house and is elemental." The building's messages tell us not only that it is a house (conforming to A. W. N. Pugin's principle that "A building should look like the kind of building it is"), but also that it is a sheltering, cozy, homey sort of house (conforming to Adolf Loos's idea that "Architecture arouses moods in us. Therefore it is the task of the architect to make this mood precise."), and also that it eschews conventional abstraction (conventional, at least, for an architect-designed house in 1964) in favor of more traditional, even vernacular forms and decoration.

A less obvious example of intentional connotative meaning is the Goddard Library in Worcester, Massachusetts, designed by John Jo-

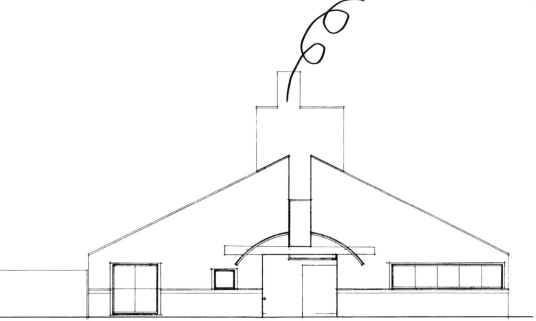

Robert Venturi's house for his mother, Chestnut Hill, Pennsylvania: Meant to remind the observer of a stereotype house, it is indeed similar to the sort of house a child might draw. (Photograph: Rollin La France, courtesy Robert Venturi; illustration: courtesy Robert Venturi)

143

John Johansen's Goddard Library, Worcester, Massachusetts: "Like the rear, not the tidy front, of a Xerox copier." (Photograph: George Cserna)

hansen in the mid-sixties. About such design, Johansen wrote in *The American Scholar* that "The overwhelming presence of electronic devices will lead to a degree of imitation in our buildings. . . . Interchangeability of parts with different circuit patterns for various performances may suggest that very different building types . . . will be assembled of different combinations of the same components" and that there will be, in general, an influence on esthetic content "governed by conscious awareness of our changing technology and environment." This goal of investing architecture with the characteristics of the electronic age was an ambitious and adventurous one, and it seems that Johansen largely succeeded. Certainly the library looks, in Johansen's own words from *Architectural Forum*, "like the rear, not the tidy front of a Xerox copier, with the components and their connections rigged on a structural chassis and exposed." Whether such a goal, requiring the jettisoning of a normal degree of architectural order, was a worthy one is more questionable.

"Where there is no symbol and therefore no discourse, there is no art," according to Sir Herbert Read. If a building is to be appreciated by us as architecture, it must speak to us and we must listen. But we must discriminate between the quack of the duck and the richer, more

abstract language of which architecture is capable. We must also c
criminate between those meanings that are truly inherent in built fo
and those we bring to it. A young English art historian, David Watkin,
in *The Rise of Architectural History,* has discussed how identical forms
may be given conflicting interpretations. Baroque church interiors,
for those on the continent of Europe, were clear symbols of Roman
Catholicism and of absolute monarchy; for some who adopted them
in England in the late seventeenth century, they came to symbolize
the opposite, the cause of the Whigs and the Protestants. We ourselves
are part of any discourse, certainly, and symbols, like words, mean
whatever we agree they will mean, but still we should avoid the fallacy
of attributing too literal meanings to built forms. The baroque genuinely connotes movement and perhaps even passion, but it directly
connotes neither Catholicism nor Protestantism. Nor is a pointed arch
inherently Christian, as Geoffrey Scott has explained. These are associations, not meanings.

Where meaning ends and association begins is, admittedly, elusive.
Similarly, it is difficult to separate what buildings mean from what
we know them to be. Perhaps at the highest level of the building art,
we would be unable to make any distinction between means and ends,
between medium and message. In the perfect work the content would
be so inherent, so intimately engaged by structure and mass, that the
building and its meaning would be indivisible. "All art aspires to the
condition of music," Pater said (a much more precise remark than
Leonardo's calling music the sister of painting or Schelling's talk-
ing about frozen music). "For while in all other kinds of art it is possible to distinguish the matter from the form, and the understanding
can always make the distinction, yet it is the constant effort of art to
obliterate it." And Claude Mauriac, writing in *The New Literature,*
gave us a statement about fiction that is easily applicable to architecture: "Creative artists have always been preoccupied with technical
questions. But form is distinct from content only in unsuccessful
works."

Here, of course, we are thinking only of content that is both serious
and abstract. The garland chiseled over the window will always remain
on the surface of architecture; it may be charming, but it is literal and
trivial. What we would hope to see well integrated with the form that
conjures it up is a significance. It will be a significance that cannot
be completely captured in words, that, indeed, can be fully expressed
in no medium other than architecture, but that is, even so, immediately identifiable. To be untranslatable is not to be unclear, and
the clarity of architectural meaning rests on architectural order.

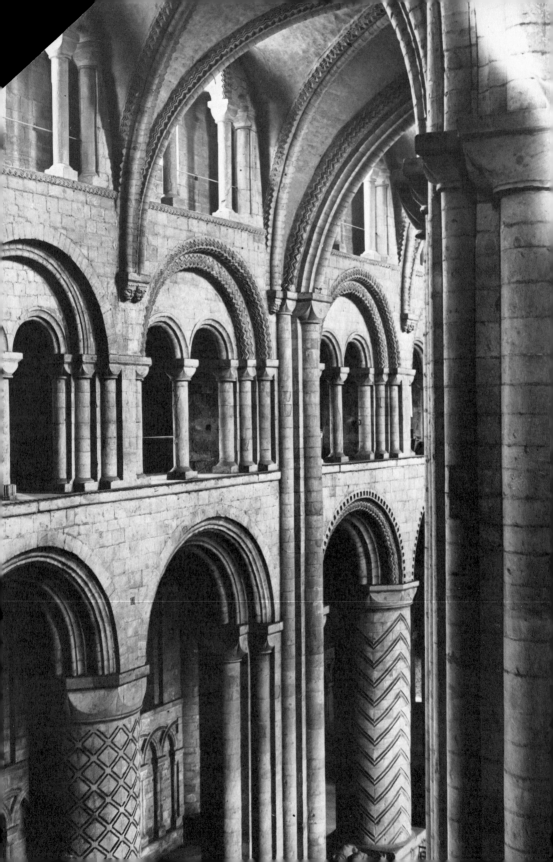

Architectural Order

If in the first act of a play a rifle is seen hanging on the wall,
it has to shoot in the last act.

Attributed to Chekov

On the other hand,

The less likely an event is to happen, the more information
does its occurrence represent.

Rudolf Arnheim, Entropy and Art

and

The only cats worth anything are the cats who take chances.
Sometimes I play things I never heard myself.

Attributed to Thelonius Monk

Much has already been said here about order. The reasoned
relationships of parts to parts, of parts to wholes, of buildings to places,
the power of repetition and modularity, the perception of complete units,
the expression of construction realities, and the signification of inherent meaning—all are born only of order, not of chance. The logical
ordering of design is at the heart of an architect's task.

Durham Cathedral: The repetition of structurally equivalent bays is more satisfying than if each were an independent invention; within this logical repetition,
however, the variation of patterns on the piers is quite welcome. (Photograph:
National Monuments Record, London)

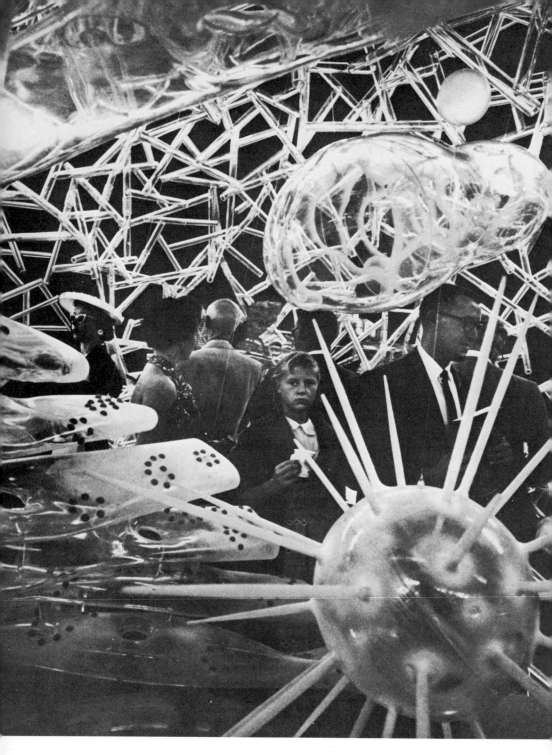

A greatly enlarged model of a human cell: What we might see lacks the quality we recognize as visual order. (Courtesy The Upjohn Co.)

Not that there can be in any work of art, nor, indeed, in any work of man that has a reasonable degree of complexity about it, such a thing as absolute order. If ever we were to discover it, we would find it stiff and lifeless. Neither can there be such a thing as a work that is formless or completely disordered, for then we would be unable to distinguish it as a work. ("Form," according to poet Richard Blackmur, "is the limiting principle by which a thing is itself.") Architecture, then, must lie somewhere between total order and disorder, between homogeneity and chaos. In the structure of nature, according to metallurgist/philosopher Cyril Stanley Smith, "hierarchy becomes inevitable in all systems excepting only those that are completely ordered or completely disordered, for these have no levels between the units and the whole assembly." In architecture, too, hierarchy—or some other sort of organization—is needed to relate the units to the whole assembly and to make of all the parts together something perceptible as a unit.

Even though structural order must exist in nature, however, nature cannot be made to serve as a model for architectural order. In the universe as a whole, the malign rule of entropy condemns us to increasing chaos (or so it seems to most scientists, at least; others suspect a loophole in the Second Law of Thermodynamics that permits local systems to run uphill against the flow to disorder), while at cellular and atomic scale, what we might see lacks recognizable order. Of course, our own existence is proof that the strictest cellular order must prevail, but it is not of the sort that looks, to our eyes and minds, like order. Goethe, in an essay "On German Architecture," praised "mother Nature, who despises and hates the inappropriate and the unnecessary." Alas, she doesn't; even at our own scale, much of her work is capricious, paradoxical, whimsical, or messy. Spendthrift nature is careless about boundaries, and boundaries are essential to works of art. Aristotle's thoughts about artistic economy are well known:

As in the other arts, so in poetry the object is a unit; therefore, in a tragedy, the plot, representing an organically united action, must be an identical whole, the structural order of the incidents being such that transposing or removing any one of them will dislocate and disorganize the whole: for a thing whose presence or absence makes no perceptible difference is not an organic part of the whole.

Matisse said something very similar: "All that is not useful in the picture is detrimental." So we may think of artistic order as a creation opposed to nature, a product of human planning in the face of the haphazard. Art is evidence of man's triumph over nature.

Man-made order need not be unnaturally regimented, however. There are many ways to order elements other than putting them in straight lines. In some compositions, only an overriding personal taste, if distinct enough, can convey a sense that the assembled elements belong together. This sort of taste unifies the profusion of shapes, spaces, and objects in Sir John Soane's intricate puzzle of a London town house, now (and since 1833, four years before his death) a museum. It consists of one structure built for himself by Soane in 1792 and two others he added later. The central one spreads itself, in the back, to encompass the width of the whole trio, its spaces and floors opening to each other with a remarkable variety of vistas, both horizontal and vertical, all elaborated with domes, niches, mirrors, and series of hinged planes that open or close to reveal different groups of paintings or objects—all this being crammed with busts, urns, marble fragments, sarcophagi, pottery, casts, and a collection of 30,000 architectural drawings. Yet there is not a square foot in this complex that is not indentifiably Soane's.

In quite a different vein is the rambling handmade house in Woodstock, New York, patched together bit by bit by Clarence Schmidt, who has been described both as "one of the paradigms of the grass roots movement" and as "the first beatnik." Schmidt's house is made from odd timbers, old windows, fragments of mirrors, aluminum pie plates, bicycle wheels, tarred lumber and dead limbs, much of it vis-

A view of the Dome Room and a section through Sir John Soane's Museum, London: Crowded, elaborate, profuse, yet it retains a coherent identity. (Photograph: The Trustees of Sir John Soane's Museum; illustration: The Trustees of Sir John Soane's Museum)

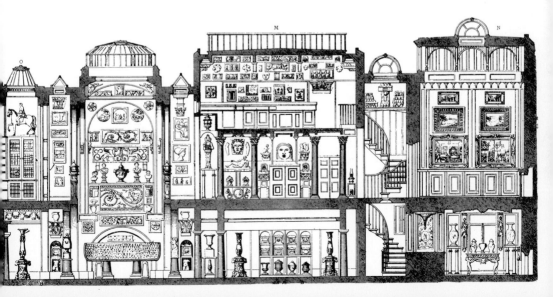

Clarence Schmidt's handmade house, Woodstock, New York: Cohesion through the force of intense idiosyncrasy. (Photograph: Greg Blasdel)

ually transformed by being wrapped in a crinkly, reflective layer of aluminum foil; it is held together as a recognizable whole by the same degree of personal idiosyncrasy.

Even in the case of the buildings of savages, Goethe wrote in the same nature-praising essay, "the most arbitrary and incongruous forms and lines" were harmonious because "a unity of feeling created out of them a characteristic whole." Architectural order need not be an order we are familiar with, then; it can be highly personal to the artist and, for the observer, completely new.

A special case, one might think, is the creation of an architectural whole from elements that are not themselves architecture but other arts. Ruskin, at his most perverse, claimed that "the fact is, there are only two fine arts possible to the human race, sculpture and painting. What we call architecture is only the association of these in noble masses, or the placing them in fit places." Not far removed from this extreme view was the general view of the whole Victorian era that architecture could be art, but only when it was fancied up with the help of sculpture and painting. A nineteenth-century observer of the Crystal Palace, for example, complained that "it has not a sufficient amount of decoration about its parts to take it entirely out of the category of first-class engineering, and to make it entirely an object of Fine Art." Yet when carvings and frescoes are subsumed in a complete and harmonious building, the total product is no other art than architecture, so that, if there is to be any further squabbling about relative primacy among the arts, we might well put our bets on architecture. "The only safe assertion," however, as Susanne Langer wrote in *Problems of Art*, "is that every work has its primary apparition, to which all other virtual dimensions are secondary. There are no happy marriages in art—only successful rape."

We inform architecture with logic so that it becomes available for our own use, not only as a perceptible visual object, but also as a practical one. As Georges Gromort taught his students at the École des Beaux-Arts, "One never need ask the way in a properly designed building." Not, at least, unless the architect intends for you to be lost, which is rarely, but sometimes, the case. The maze has served as model for some children's play structures, such as Studio BBPR's labyrinth for the tenth Triennale in Milan, and architect Aldo van Eyck has given this explanation of his Arnheim exhibition pavilion: "Central to my idea was that the structure should not reveal what happens inside until one gets quite close, approaching it from ends. Bump!—sorry. What's this? Oh Hello!"

Sometimes we can be thoroughly delighted by building parts for which an overall view of the whole left us unprepared. Piranesi's only building, the church of Santa Maria del Priorata, Rome, is an example. Seen from the foot of the Aventine, its white marble facade, although dramatically punctured by a bull's-eye window, appears sedate, proper, perhaps even a little austere. At the top of the hill, close enough to see the details of the facade, the impression of austerity is forgotten. As we might have expected, the facade incorporates references not only to the iconography of Christianity in general but also of the church's patrons, the Knights of Malta, in particular. But there are completely unexpected details, too. Plaques interrupting the fluting of the four giant pilasters carry, it had seemed from far away, reliefs of crosses; seen close up, they are cross-shaped assemblages of weapons and relics: From a distance, the four seemed identical; close up, each is unique. And these pilasters have the volutes of their capitals

Piranesi's only building, the little church of Santa Maria del Priorata, Rome: From a distance, proper and austere, but, seen at close range, the details of its facade writhe with the fantasies of the architect's imagination. (Photographs: Stanley Abercrombie)

formed by the hindquarters of griffins. What had looked like scrolls are coiled serpents. When a row of dentils changes direction, the corner dentil is replaced by a pine cone. The facade, in fact, writhes with products of Piranesi's fantastic imagination, and these products possess special interest simply because they were disguised from those who viewed the facade only from afar. Broadcast, these fantasies might have palled or even repelled; whispered only to the church's intimates, they fascinate.

So there is a place for the unexpected, and logic need not eliminate surprise. Yet logic and surprise are often at odds. How is this conflict to be resolved, and which surprises can be said to be supportive of, which ones destructive of order?

Let us try to imagine the unimaginable: an absolutely neutral building. It is neither a good building nor a bad one. In size, it is big enough to be recognizable as having serviceable internal capacity, but not so big as to be imposing. In shape, it is a simple rectangular solid, reasonably proportioned. Its sides and roof are perfectly flat, and its corners are right angles. It sits on level ground. Its door is centered on one long face, the most natural location, for it is at the point of the building exterior closest to the building center, from which all parts of the interior are easily accessible. Its window openings are regularly spaced. Its color is a flat, pale gray. It is so featureless that nothing can be read of its structure or of its construction materials. It is respectable, but obviously without interest.

But now let us imagine conditions that our dull little building might respond to. A sloping site may demand an irregular base; snow loads may require a pitched roof; the location of a parking lot at one side of the building may suggest that the entrance be shifted toward the nearest corner, and this shift will, in turn, alter the interior circulation system. Soil conditions may demand special spans and exotic structural devices. Internal functions—our little building may enclose a cyclotron, or a rare book library, or perhaps a family of giraffes—will necessarily produce effects that are far from neutral. Many of these effects, when we first come upon our transformed building, will surprise us: Windows high enough so that giraffes can see out of them will appear strange on the building's exterior. But only at first, for when we come

Top, the regular patterns of ribs of the vault of Canterbury Cathedral speak of a resolute architectural order; *bottom,* the syncopated pattern of Lincoln, however, introduces a personal element that is interesting but distracting and somewhat disturbing. (Photographs: National Monuments Record, London)

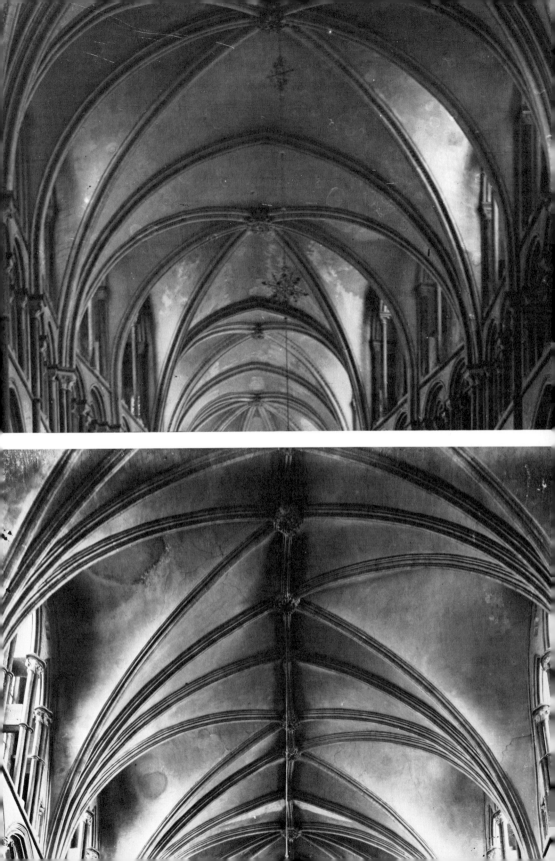

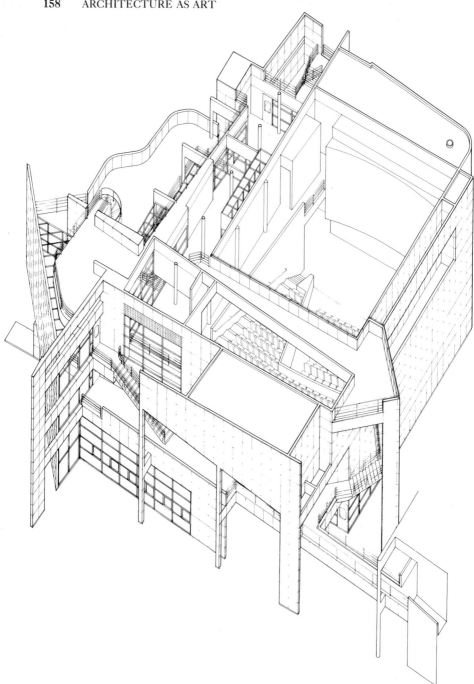

Richard Meier's Atheneum, New Harmony, Indiana: We read what we can, and we credit as legible even that part we cannot read. (Courtesy Richard Meier)

to know the building's determinants, they will cease to surprise; they will, in fact, explain the building to us. Art historian Judith Wechsler, in her introduction to *On Aesthetics in Science,* speaks of "the 'Aha' that accompanies the discovery of a connection or an unexpected but utterly right realization in art and science." And this is the response our logically determined surprises will evoke: Our initial "Oh?" will become "Aha!"

The same response can come from surprises that answer more personal and less practical requirements, that are artistic manipulations to intensify the building's connotative meanings or to express some intangible artistic urge. Architecture can be taken very far indeed toward disorder; it can be so laden with surprise that our eyes can find no place to rest, and yet the strength of the underlying artistic impulse can still dominate. So long as we feel confident that the architect is in control and that his effects are intentional, we can accept them as meaningful.

Richard Meier's Atheneum in New Harmony, Indiana, presents us, at first sight, with a bewildering display of effects—fins, screens, ramps, stairs, overhangs and undercuts, curves and angles. As we study the building, particularly as we move through it, we come to understand that the entire structure is a machine for displaying information about New Harmony, that its general form corresponds to the process of our progressing through, around, and even over it. We see at one point a model of the town, at another a display of local artifacts, at another a brief film about the town's history, at yet another a rooftop view of the town, and, finally, at the end of our preparation, we are directed down a long ramp leading to New Harmony itself. We realize also, then, that many of the complexities that seemed arbitrary or mysterious are really quite sensibly related to this circulation.

Other complexities in the form of the Atheneum have resulted from a logic that has been established not by Meier's response to the demands of circulation, but by his response to the very idea of construction. This response was in the form of an abstract (and necessarily inexact) concept of how the building might be organized. Throughout the design process, from commission to completed construction, this concept—subject at each step to some alteration—served as the guide to which all design decisions were referred.

All architects work with some such concept, of course; architecture is too complex ever to be done, with success, in any *ad hoc* manner. In the case of Clarence Schmidt's handmade palace of mirrored fragments and foil, the concept must have been something no more specific than a vision of something extensive and glittering. For the

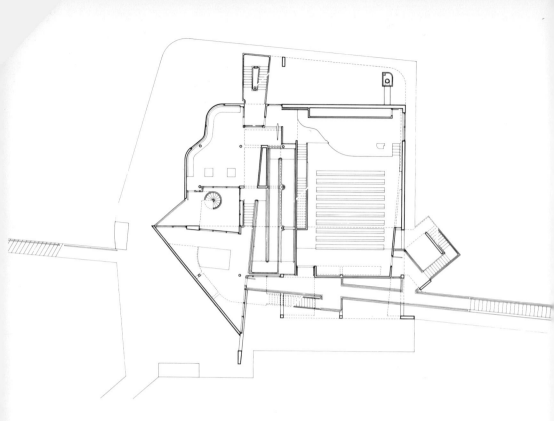

The Atheneum's plan is based not on one simple right-angled grid, but on several such grids superimposed, and one corner of the plan—facing the Wabash River—has been allowed to curve, free of any grid alignment. (Courtesy Richard Meier)

Greeks, it was a shared set of fixed rules governing the relationships between all building elements. For a simple warehouse today, it may be a structural grid; for an office interior, it may be a module based on the size and shape of work stations. But always, at the heart of a well-designed building, is a concept. As the critic Claude Bragdon wrote earlier this century, "A work of architecture may be significant, organic, dramatic, but it will fail to be a work of art unless it be also *schematic*. It means (this word) a systematic disposition of parts according to some co-ordinating principle."

In the case of the Atheneum, Meier's concept, we can infer from what is built, was something like this: Basic to the building, as it had been to the existing town of New Harmony (and as it is, indeed, to most buildings and to many towns), would be an orthogonal grid of mutually perpendicular elements. However, just as the long ramp would be allowed to cut diagonally down through the building mass, so would it (and some related elements) be allowed to cut at a five-degree angle through the building plan's thicket of right-angled elements. And, finally, the edge of the building away from the town and facing the sinuous banks of the Wabash River would itself be allowed to undulate like a river bank, free of any grid alignments.

When we see the Atheneum, then, we are able to understand some of its complexities, as we have said, as consequences of the circulation pattern that is the key to its functions, and we are able to understand other complexities as consequences of Meier's building concept. The Atheneum is an unusually intricate building, but not at all a disorderly one.

Even so, some parts of the building may still puzzle us. But partly because we have come to see that many parts are intelligible and reasonable, partly because they are presented with fine surfaces and polished details and are therefore convincing in manner, and partly because, diverse as they are, they share a single formal vocabulary we can recognize as the architect's voice—for all these reasons, we acknowledge the building's authority as art. We read what we can, and we credit as legible even that part we cannot read.

Stanley Tigerman's Illinois Regional Library for the Blind and the Physically Handicapped, on the near west side of Chicago, is a much simpler building than the Atheneum, but it, too, presents us with some elements that seem at first inexplicable. The window in one facade, for example, is a continuous slit with its upper edge rippling like a roller coaster. It is a felicitous, playful, pleasing shape, but we wonder immediately about the pull of gravity on this construction; only in our own age of steel-reinforced masonry could a wall be sliced in such a manner and still stand; in timber or in load-bearing stone it would have been impossible. And this structural accomplishment would be an empty extravagance if there were no reason, other than whimsy, for wanting it built. There being no clues on the exterior, we look inside. Here we find that the window wall is paralleled by a long counter for library services, and that the counter is curved in plan just as the window is in elevation. This is an architectural element for the blind to read; its easily remembered eccentricities of shape tell them where they are along the counter's length. Changes in counter height, in addition, mark those places where patrons in wheelchairs can be served, as opposed to the lengths of higher counter against which they can only wait in line. For those who are partially sighted, the rising and falling of the long window produces detectable changes in the level of light, giving them another aid for orientation. And, of course, the window is an exterior expression of interior char-

Stanley Tigerman's Illinois Regional Library for the Blind and Physically Handicapped, Chicago: The long, rippling window is a felicitous but questionable shape, until we learn of its close relationship to the configuration of the counter beyond it, its undulations making it "readable"by the blind.(Photographs : Howard N. Kaplan, courtesy Stanley Tigerman)

acter; it has been created, with some effort, not just to ornament a surface but also to convey some meaning.

But other surprises in other buildings betray a loss of control. If, to our neutral building, curiously high windows were added with no giraffes to look out of them, or if long ramps were added that led nowhere, or if the entrance, through some builder's error, were tilted a few degrees from the vertical, or if a gallon of bright green paint were spilled over one corner—then we would be left with an "Oh?" that never could become "Aha!"

We must discriminate, therefore, between these two sorts of surprises: those that convey information and those that don't. The first sort always constitutes an improvement over uncommunicative neutrality; the second sort degrades neutrality toward disorder. Thus order is not opposed to surprise, only to meaningless surprise.

But what of Thelonius Monk's admiration, quoted at the beginning of this chapter, for "the cats who take chances"? Can the architect take similar chances and succeed? Certainly, for the chances Monk meant are not accidents, but intuitive leaps that are founded on talent and experience. And even accidents, in the music of John Cage and others and in the quick work of every good watercolorist, can be incorporated into perceptible and delightful compositions, even though such work may tread dangerously near the edge beyond which meaning is lost. Architecture, we have said, must have a meaning, even if it is an untranslatable one, and logical order in architecture is not an end, but a means of clarifying that meaning and making it perceptible.

Conclusion: Three Relationships

"And when I found the door was locked,
I pulled and pushed and kicked and knocked.
And when I found the door was shut,
I tried to turn the handle, but . . ."
There was a long pause.
"Is that all?" Alice timidly asked.
"That's all," said Humpty Dumpty. "Goodbye."

Lewis Carroll, *Through the Looking-Glass*

We have tried to shake apart the various aspects of architecture so that we could examine its art unencumbered by its practical responsibilities. This has been only a partial success. We may have found that the attachments between, say, beauty and function are less binding than popular slogans have told us, but we have never quite been able to catch sight of the art of architecture in immaculate isolation.

What has become apparent, instead, is that there are three relationships that have surfaced continually, sometimes only suggested, sometimes quite explicit. They are not unrelated to architecture's utilitarian tasks, for they are basic both to those tasks and to esthetic excellence. If art and use are considered as parallel products of these relationships, we see that use is not a product of art, nor art a product of use. These two broad aspects of architecture are not unrelated, then, but they are related as siblings, not as mutual dependents.

The Union League, Philadelphia: We do not need to see a figure on the stair to understand what the shape is suggesting to us, nor do we need to distinguish between the accommodation of movement and the celebration of movement; there is both. (Photograph: Julie Jensen)

September and February views of part of William Strickland's Second Bank of the United States, Philadelphia: A building is most alive when it exhibits change. (Photographs: Julie Jensen)

The three relationships at the heart of architecture are that of a building to the earth, of a building to man, and of a building to itself.

By relating to the earth, we mean that a building must acknowledge, in some perceptible way, the size and power of the earth. The most obvious manifestation of the earth's power is gravity, and no building becomes architecture without conveying some sense of gravity. That sense may be demonstrated by a visible concession to its pull, or by a visible reaction against it, by the sturdy mass of a ziggurat, the insouciant acrobatics of a tensile structure, the calm calculation of post and beam, the sweep of an arch, or the bravado of a cantilever.

Gravity, of course, is not the only force the earth exerts. Others—wind, rain, lightning, volcanoes, earthquakes—sweep over its face and erupt beneath us. Architecture is an art that cannot be packed away when conditions are difficult; it must be appropriate for all seasons, all times of day, all types of lighting, all weather. Like the response to gravity, the response to these conditions can be made into a visual, as well as a practical, asset. A building is most alive when it exhibits change, when the patterns of its shadows reflect the seasons,

and when, over many years, its weathering and staining occur so that we know they were expected and planned for.

The earth's spinning and orbiting vary the light that falls on our buildings, and one of architecture's greatest potentials for delight is the way it displays itself through such variations. One of photography's shortcomings in presenting architecture is that it cannot convey these changes. "Our eyes are made to see forms in light," Le Corbusier wrote. "Light and shade reveal these forms."

Architecture must also relate to the earth by exhibiting an awareness of earthly resources and their relative values. This requires a sense of worth as well as a sense of cost, for the most economical solution is not always the best, and neither is the most costly. Opulence is often called for, but a sense of waste spoils our admiration for art.

The relationship of building to man is more complex. At the simplest level, this is a matter of size and shape. All building elements—rooms, doors, doorknobs, and a thousand others—must be designed with an awareness of the physical characteristics of the users. In this respect architecture differs fundamentally from sculpture. We may walk inside some sculpture just as we would walk into a building, but the sculptural space does not need to house an activity. Even a sculpture that has the human figure as its subject matter need not be life-size. The building-man relationship is a correspondence, not a representation.

Considerably more subtle are the ways in which buildings relate to man's psychological state. They do so by manipulating that state, by inducing reactions of release, claustrophobia, rectitude, pomp, security, festivity, and so on. Buildings can also embody and reflect both physical and psychological states. Geoffrey Scott said of the classic and Renaissance styles that "the centre of that architecture was the human body; its method, to transcribe in stone the body's favourable states; and the moods of the spirit took visible shape along its borders, power and laughter, strength and terror and calm."

Sometimes architecture manipulates states and embodies them simultaneously, and sometimes it is hard to say which it is doing. But it is at its best when some sort of rapport with human form, human movement, and the human condition is evident. A stair can bring us from one floor to the next with mere efficiency, while another can sweep us from floor to floor with great flair. We do not need to see a human figure using the stair to understand what the stair is saying to us; in our minds, we see ourselves there. Nor do we need to distinguish between the accommodation of movement and the celebration of movement; there is both.

Such an attitude toward human users is something we detect in the work of the very best architects, and it is something not at all equivalent to mere function. Frank Lloyd Wright's architecture (for all his writing to the contrary) was not, at heart, particularly concerned with function, yet it exhibited this attitude toward users to an exceptional degree. His houses, George Nelson once wrote in *Fortune,* "enclose space as if it were precious not for the sake of the space itself, but for the life that goes on within it."

If they are to produce architecture, buildings and building elements must also be designed with an awareness of their users' perception. The architect must know exactly how his building will be seen. A building with a reentrant (or concave) corner occurring above a salient (or convex) corner is a case of a form that is visually indeterminate: Not being able to see where the upper form meets the lower, we are unable to judge precisely its size or even its location. The architect may have reasons for wanting to produce such a disturbing effect, but he should not produce disturbance unintentionally.

Architecture must also be aware of its users as fellow actors against the backdrop of nature. The pairing of man and building is inevitable, and the relationship only awaits proper expression. Despite its size, architecture is man's more intimately than any other art, for man apprehends it not as a remote object but as a close accomplice in his own reality. Man shares his world with buildings, not by choice but by necessity.

We have said that architecture is both a utility and a communication, both of the world and about the world. It is more: It *is* a world. Every successful work of architecture is a new and coherent whole. New, no matter how similar to how many other buildings, because it is a unique creation that has been brought into being in its own particular time and place. Coherent, because we must be able to understand its meaning and also because, in another sense of the word, it must hold together, part to part and parts within the whole.

This is the third relationship, then, the relationship of a building to itself. More than the first two, it is a relationship shared by the other arts; even here, though, architecture has some special ways, for our apprehension of building detail has a timing unlike that of our seeing brushstrokes in a painting (always after we have seen the whole painting) or the passages in a novel or symphony (always serially, before we have any knowledge of the whole). Architecture and its constituent details coexist for us. We cannot predict which will be seen first; we can only say that this art cannot be comprehended until we have developed some knowledge of both the whole and its parts and understand that they belong together.

Having isolated three relationships that are particularly important keys to the art of architecture, we are left with the final question of how to use these keys. For architects, they are relationships to be considered in the process of design. For observers of architecture, they are relationships to be questioned in the process of evaluation. We can say that a work of architecture is a building that successfully deals with all three of them. If a work fails in any of these ways, it must fail, at least partly, as art.

No building needs to be spectacular and certainly no building needs to be original in its resolution of any of the three. (Although a building that is absolutely taciturn in its approach to all three is likely to be taciturn indeed.) What is needed is not relationships that startle or impress but relationships that convince. And what they must convince us of is simply that they have been investigated and resolved. To be convincing, of course, the resolutions must be clearly communicated; in this, no arcane references, self-indulgent tricks, or private jokes will suffice. There is a place for jokes and indirection, but it is a place nearer the surface of art, playing a less critical role. Certainly there is ample proof from other arts that serious esthetic achievement can be presented with a lighthearted, even a flippant tone—*Cosi fan tutte*, for example, or *The Importance of Being Earnest*. Art need not be dour, but, in its fundamentals, it needs to be sincere.

Our three relationships can be resolved in the most simple and straightforward ways. In some cases (in the relationship of building to earth, for example, when the building and earth are both devoid of irregularity or eccentricity), the simple and straightforward relationship is the only one that *can* convince us. In other cases, the architect can only succeed by means of a surprising, unpredicted, and bold leap of the imagination. This latter approach produces the most exciting architecture, of course, but there is a temptation that the architect must avoid in choosing this path: He must not pretend to solve problems when none exists. A great leap across a chasm is thrilling; a great leap across a level field is a waste of energy. Having raised our expectations by calling attention to a dramatic event, the architect must leave us with more information, not less, than we previously expected. His surprises, as we have said, must leave us not asking "Oh?" but saying "Aha!"

To suggest three relationships as the keys to the process of raising building to the level of architecture is obviously not equivalent to offering a three-ingredient recipe that the architect can follow for sure esthetic success, nor a three-question test that the observer can apply for the identification of such success. For something as complicated as architecture, no such shortcuts could be credible.

Therefore, despite all our efforts at common sense, we leave the subject of architecture, as we came to it, a subject with an element of mystery. In the process of design, the architect confronts a multitude of competing and often conflicting demands. How he makes the decisions, sometimes studiously, sometimes in an inspired instant, that will simultaneously satisfy several of these demands while denying none of them—that remains a mystery of the creative mind. The creative process, unlike the scientific process, produces results that are not specified in advance; we cannot expect to find complete directions toward a goal that is unpredictable.

How we respond to the architect's work is similarly mysterious. There are logical processes of looking at architecture, and our looking will be better informed if we know them and have practiced them, if, first of all, we discriminate between the esthetics of a building and its many other attributes, and then discriminate between fundamental form and surface embellishments. Yet, however well informed, our acceptance or rejection of architecture is often spontaneous; by mental processes far quicker than any conscious logic, we can know imme-diately that one building is good, another bad.

So there remains in the art of architecture something that evades analysis, something that touches us in the most secret parts of our minds, something not only beyond utility but also beyond all that is rational and everyday. It could not be otherwise for our biggest, toughest, most complex, most permanent, and most powerful art.

INDEX

Aalto, Alvar, 37, 132
Aida, Takefumi, Nirvana House, *140*
Alberti, Leone Battista, 67, 72
    Palazzo Ruccellai, 120
Allen, Gerald, 123
Ames, Anthony, *84*
Ammanati, Pitti Palace, 131, *132*, 133
Andagna, Italy, *94*
Apollo 12 spacecraft, *101*
Aristotle, 149
Arithmetic and architecture, 76, 78–80,
    82–84
Arnheim, Rudolf, 147
Art Nouveau architecture, 136
Atheneum, New Harmony, Indiana, *158*,
    159, 160–161
Aurelian Wall, 17, 19

Baker's Monument, *61*
Barberini, 136
BBPR, 153
Beach house, *62*, *69*
Belvedere, St. Peter's, *139*
Bernini, 90
Blackmur, Richard, 149
Blake, Peter, 125
Bofill, Ricardo, Parc de la Marca Hispanica,
    38
Boswell, 101
Boullée, Étienne-Louis, 50
    interior by, *19*
Bowen, Elizabeth, 17, 19
Bragdon, Claude, 160
Bramante, Tempietto, 31
Brazen Palace, *32*
Breuer, Marcel, 102
    IBM headquarters, *128*
    Robinson House, *91*
    Whitney Museum, 10

Brolin, Brent, 96
Brown, Denise Scott, 125
Brownlee house, *106*
Brunelleschi
    Foundling Hospital, 99
    Pazzi Chapel, 31
Burke, Edmund, 19, 22
Burlington, Lord, 102, 119

Cage, John, 163
Cambridge University building, *21*
Canter, David, 104
Canterbury Cathedral, *157*
Cantilever, 108, 110
Capital, Sant'Antimo, *139*
Cardano, Geronimo, 67
Carpenter, Rhys, 45, 110
Carroll, Lewis, 165
Carved architecture, 90
Casa del Fascio, 127
Casinos, 130–131
Cathedrals
    Gothic, 59, 60, 105, 107
    medieval, 126–127
Cell, human, *148*
Chaitkin, William, 10
Chakravarty, Subhash, 96
Chandigarh, 96
Chekhov, attributed to, 147
Chesterton, G. K., 127
Chiesa delle Maddalena, *93*
Chiswick House, 119, *120*
Church of the Redeemer, *88*
Churches, 130–131, 145
Cioran, E. M., 117
Climatron, St. Louis Botanical Garden, *23*
Cloister of the Duomo, *126*
"Cloud Props" project, 112, *113*
Cogan House, *45*

Coleman Young Recreation Center, 63, *64*
Columns, papyrus, *124*
Constructional functionalism, 112–113
Coppedé, Gino, building, *49*
Crystal Palace, 153

Day, D. H., farm, *130*
De Zurko, Robert, 101, 102
di Giorgi, Francesco, 67
Dome, 23, 40–41
Drew, Jane, 96
Dulles Airport, 129
Duomo
     Lucca, *47*, 48
     Sicily, *126*
Dürer, Albrecht, *73*
Durham Cathedral, 48, *146*

Egypt, ancient, 11, 71
Ehrenkrantz, Ezra, number grid, *60*
Empson, William, 51–52
Engine test-cell building, 113–114
Environment and architecture, 87–98,
     166, 167
Euclid, 76, 133

Farm of D. H. Day, *130*
Farnese, 136
Ferri, Roger C., design for pedestrian city,
     81, *138*
Fibonacci series, 82
Fitch, James Marston, 11
Fontana, Carlo, *30*
Frankel, Paul T., 76
Fry, Maxwell, 96
Fry, Roger, 133
Fukuoka Mutual Bank, *66*
Fuller, Buckminster, 19, 23, 62
     Climatron, St. Louis Botanical Garden,
     23
Functionalist theories, 101–104
Functions of architecture, 99–116
Funerary complex, Egypt, *39*

Galileo, 23, 76
Gas refinery, Michigan, *33*
Gatje, Robert, IBM headquarters, *128*
Gazebo, Cairo Citadel, *98*
Geodesic dome, 23
George Washington Bridge, *22*
Gilbert, Cass, 22
Giorgini, Vittorio, structure, *22*, 23
Goddard Library, 142, 144, *144*
Goethe, 149, 152

Goldsmith, Myron, 24–25
     graph of bridge structures, *24*
Gothic cathedrals, 59–60, 105, 107
Gravity, 166, 167
Great Pyramid of Cheops, *16*, 71
Greek architecture, ancient, 47, 110, 160
Greenough, Horatio, 47
Gromort, Georges, 153
Gropius, Walter, 100
Grotto, park in Italy, *86*
Guggenheim Museum, *122*, 123

Hadrian's Villa, *116*
Hambridge, Jay, 80
Helmholtz, von, 69
Hitchcock, Henry-Russell, 113
"Honolulu House," *109*
Horta, Victor, Van Eetvelde house, *137*
Human body and architecture, 72, 74–76,
     167–168
Hunt, Richard Morris, Fifth Avenue front of
     Metropolitan Museum of Art, 56–57, *57*
Hutcheson, Francis, 102, 117
Huxtable, Ada Louise, 31

IBM headquarters, France, *128*
Illinois Regional Library for the Blind and
     Physically Handicapped, 161, *162*, 163
Industrial buildings, 113–114
Isozaki, Arata
     Fukuoka Mutual Bank, *66*
     museum, 63, *65*
Izenour, Steven, 125

James, Henry, 8, 138
Japanese house, 62–63, *63*
Jefferson, Thomas, 119
     Rotunda, *41*, 100–101
Jencks, Charles, 10, 52
Johansen, John, Goddard Library, 142, 144,
     144
John Hancock Center, 110, *111*
Johnson & Johnson buildings, New Jersey,
     129
Johnson, Philip, 104, 113
     Seagram Building, 95
Johnson Wax headquarters, 129

Kahn, Louis
     Kimbell Art Museum, 45, *46*
     Yale Center for British Art, *83*
Kallen, Horace, 104
Kant, 104, 119
Kaufmann, Edgar, jr., 7–8

Keats, 127
Kessler, William, 63
    Coleman Young Recreation Center, *64*
Khan, Fazlur, 110
Kimbell Art Museum, 45, *46*
Kitt Peak Observatory, *14*

Landscape, see Environment
Langer, Susanne, 7, 153
Laugier, Marc Antoine, 48
Le Corbusier, 41, 102, 114, 118, 127, 167
    Chandigarh, 96
    La Tourette monastery, 126
    Modulor system, 79, 82–84, *84*
    on music and architecture, 70–71
    Toward a New Architecture, 17
Leonardo, 74, 145
Lethaby, W. R., 48, 130
Lever House, 129
Lissitzky, El, "Cloud Props" project, 112, *113*
Location and architecture, 87–98
Loos, Adolf, 142
L-shape, 55
Lurçat, Andre, 55
Lyndon, Donlyn, Sea Ranch Condominium, *97*

Market of Trajan, 99
Matisse, 149
Mauriac, Claude, 145
Meaning in architecture, 125–146
Medici, 146
Meier, Richard, Atheneum, *158*, 159, 160–161
Melhuish, Nigel, 135
Merchant's Exchange Building, *80*
Metropolitan Museum of Art, 56–57, *57*
Michelangelo, 25, 50
Mies van der Rohe, Ludwig, 102–103
    Barcelona pavilion, 100
    furniture, 104
    Seagram Building, 95
Millay, Edna St. Vincent, 76
Mock, Elizabeth B., 31
Modular system of Le Corbusier, 79, 82–84, *84*
Monk, Thelonius, 147, 163
Moore, Charles, 123
    Sea Ranch Condominium, California, *97*
Morris, Desmond, 122
Music and architecture, 67, 69, 70–71

Nature and architecture, 72, 74–76
Nelson, George, 168

Newman, Charles, 117
Nirvana House, *140*
Nowicki, Matthew, 96
Number grid, *60*

Obelisk, *30*, 38, 40
Order in architecture, 147–164
Orders, classical, 72, 143
Ornament, 48, 50, 51
Otto, Frei, *22*

Pacioli, Luca, 74–75
Palace of Basamtapur, *70*
Palazzo Barberini, *48*
Palazzo del Te, *28*
Palladio, 53
    Villa Capra, *134*
Panofsky, Erwin, 105, 107
Pantheon, *36*, 100
Parc de la Marca Hispanica, *38*
Parthenon, 71
Pater, Walter, 9, 50, 145
Pedestrian city, *81*, *138*
Pei, I. M., Johnson & Johnson buildings, 129
Pell's series, 78–79, 82
Perception of architecture, 117–124
Perrault, Claude, 76
Piazza Santa Cecilia, *51*
Piranesi, Church of Santa Maria del Priorata, 153, *154*, *155*, 156
Pitti Palace, 131, *132*, 133
Placement of buildings, see Environment
Plato, 102
Ponti, Gio, 99
Pope, Alexander, 102
Pratt, Abner, "Honolulu House," *109*
Pretura window, *54*
Proportioning systems
    based on:
        arithmetic, 76, 78–80, 82–84
        music, 67, 69, 70–71
        nature, 72, 74–76
        secrets of the ancients, 71
    categories of, 63, 67, *78*, *79*
    value of, 84–85
Pugin, A. W. N., 142
Pyramid, 37–38, *38*
    of Cheops, Great, *16*, 71
Pythagoras, 67

Read, Sir Herbert, 11, 28, 125, 144
Robinson House, *91*
Roman aqueduct, *114*

Roman theater, *52*, *105*
Romano, Giulio, Palazzo del Te mural, *28*
Rossi, Aldo, 96
Rubin Rubel house, *136*
Rusconi, Giovanni
    dell'Architettura, *121*
    Vitruvian figures, *74*, *75*
Ruskin, John, 15, 31, 45, 103, 115, 132,
    152–153
    on St. Peter's, 25
    Seven Lamps of Architecture, The, 17

Saarinen, Eero
    Dulles Airport, 129
    General Motors Technical Center, 113
St. Andrews University dormitories, *58*, *59*,
    133
St. George Church, *68*
St. Michael Church, *43*
St. Peter's, 25, *27*, *28*, *30*, *139*
Sanctuary, rock (India), *89*
Sansovino, Jacopo, Church of San Francesco
    della Vigna, 67
Santa Maria della Consolazione, *26*, *77*
Santa Maria della Pace, *56*
Santa Maria del Priorata, Church of, 153,
    154, *155*, 156
Schelling, Friedrich von, 7
Schmidt, Clarence, 151
    house in Woodstock, 151–152, *152*, 159
Schopenhauer, 115
Schumacher, E. F., 15
Schumacher, Thomas, 100–101
Scott, Geoffrey, 101–102, 145, 168
Scruton, Roger, 103
Sea Ranch Condominium, *97*
Seagram Building, 95
Second Bank of the United States, *166*, *167*
Sex as symbol, 38, 40
Shapes, 37–85
    dome, 40–41
    L, 55
    modular relationship of, 60, 62–63
    obelisk, *30*, 38, 40
    pyramid, 37–38, *38*
Siegel, Gwathmey
    beach house, *69*
    Cogan House, *45*
Size in architecture, 15–35
Skidmore, Owings, & Merrill
    John Hancock Tower, 110, *111*
    Kitt Peak Observatory, *14*
    Lever House, 129
Smith, Cyril Stanley, 87, 149

Smithson, Peter, 50
Soane, Sir John, 76
    London town house and museum, *150*,
    151, 151
Socrates, 102
Stam, Mart, "Cloud Props" project, 112,
    113
Stirling, James
    Cambridge University building, *21*, 22
    St. Andrews University dormitories, *58*,
    59, *133*
Stokes, Adrian, 115
Stone, Edward Durrell, 126
Strickland, William
    Merchant's Exchange Building, *80*
    Second Bank of the United States, *166*,
    167
Structural functionalism, 105, 107–108, 110,
    112
Stupa
    of Sirkap, West Pakistan, *42*
    of Swayambunath, Nepal, *141*
Sturgis, Russell, 125
Sullivan, Louis, 127
    Rubin Rubel house, *136*
Sydney Opera House, 10
Symonds, Arthur, 15

Tange, Kenzo, Yamanashi Press and Radio
    Center, *107*
Taut, Bruno, 99, 100
Teilhard de Chardin, Pierre, 117
Temple of Surya, *92*
Terragni, Guiseppe, Casa del Fascio, 127
Texture in architecture, 132–133
Thompson, Sir D'Arcy, 23–24
Thurber, James, "Home," *129*
Tigerman, Stanley, Illinois Regional Library
    for the Blind and Physically Handicapped,
    161, *162*, 163
Triora, Italy, *94*
Tsien, Billie, beach house, *62*
Turnbull, William, Sea Ranch
    Condominium, *97*

Union League, Philadelphia, *164*
Utzon, Jörn, Sydney Opera House, 10

Van Eetvelde house, *137*
van Eyck, Aldo, 9, 153
Venturi, Robert
    house for his mother, 142, *143*
    et al., *Learning from Las Vegas*, 125–126,
    129–130

Victorian house, 110
Villa Capra, *134*
Villa d'Este, 91
Villa Lante, 91
Villa Torlonia, 91
Vitruvian figures, *74, 75,* 84
Vitruvius, 71, 72
Von Foerster, Dr. Heinz, 119

Watkin, David, 145
Wechsler, Judith, 159
Wellington Memorial, Dublin, *29*
Whitaker, Robert, Sea Ranch
    Condominium, *97*
Wilde, Oscar, 130
Williams, Tod, beach house, *62*
Wimberley, Whisenand, Allison, Tong and
    Goo, Brownlee House, *106*

Wittkower, Rudolf, 67, 72, 74
Wollheim, Richard, 9
Woolworth Building, 22
World Trade Center, 31
World War II
    anti-tank defense line, *34*
    "sea forts," 110, *112*
    towers, *44*
Wright, Frank Lloyd, 25, 102, 168
    Guggenheim Museum, *122,* 123
    Johnson Wax headquarters, 129
    On Architecture, 85
    on St. Peter's, 25

Yale Center for British Art, *83*
Yamanashi Press and Radio Center, *107*

Zoser, funerary complex, *39*